D1233583

ENDORSEMENTS

We all know we're saved by faith, but then what? Using Peter as a guide, Roger Thompson gives us a powerful, biblically-based model that left me feeling more alive, more brave, more courageous, and more willing to take some big, holy risks. Amazingly, this book succeeds in walking that tightrope between compassion for the reader and a commitment to not tickle our ears—a remarkable feat in its own right. Whatever you're facing right now, I promise you will draw strength from this book. Highly recommended.

Patrick Morley,
Author of 20 books, including *The Man in the Mirror* and
Executive Chairman, Man in the Mirror

All of us—somewhere along the line—find ourselves in an extremely bad situation. In might be an emergency or crises that's been foisted upon us or just the natural consequences of our own dumb choices. Either way, if we want to have any chance of coming out of these circumstances with something to smile about it will most likely depend on what we do next. Fortunately, we can train in advance for how to confidently know what to do next, and Roger Thompson is one the best coaches we could want helping us get there. *Do the Next Right Thing* is a fast-paced, page-turning crash course in how to make common sense responses to our bigger-than-life messes.

Dr. Tim Kimmel
Author of *Grace Based Parenting* and
Grace Filled Marriage

Lying before every man is a mountain of challenge that will test him. If not now, then soon. How he navigates its face says everything about his prior preparation. You hold in your hands not a map—for each man's trail is unique—but a guidebook to steer your heart, written by a one who's helped guide many, including me, through the deep, consequential decisions to do the next right thing.

Leary Gates
Founder of BoldPath Life Strategies
President of the National Coalition of Ministries to Men

If you are looking for slick answers and quick solutions to life's challenges you won't find this in Roger Thompson's excellent book *Do The Next Right Thing*, but if you are like me, a man who wants to walk responsibly through life and make wise decisions, then this book is for you. I'm normally happy if a book or seminar gives me just one or two fresh, clear life principles that I am needing. Roger is giving us 8! You will love and learn from this excellent book. It's fascinating, practical, and fast moving.

John Yates, Sr. Pastor, The Falls Church Anglican
Author: *How a Man Prays for His Family*

DO THE NEXT RIGHT THING

To Carol,

Always, with joy, DNRT!

Roger

1 THES 5:24

EIGHT STRONG HANDHOLDS FOR EVERY MAN

DO THE NEXT RIGHT THING

ROGER THOMPSON

TATE PUBLISHING
AND ENTERPRISES, LLC

Do the Next Right Thing
Copyright © 2016 by Roger Thompson. All rights reserved.

No part of this publication may be reproduced, stored in a retrieval system or transmitted in any way by any means, electronic, mechanical, photocopy, recording or otherwise without the prior permission of the author except as provided by USA copyright law.

Scriptures taken from the *Holy Bible, New International Version*®, NIV®. Copyright © 1973, 1978, 1984 by Biblica, Inc.™ Used by permission of Zondervan. All rights reserved worldwide. www.zondervan.com

This book is designed to provide accurate and authoritative information with regard to the subject matter covered. This information is given with the understanding that neither the author nor Tate Publishing, LLC is engaged in rendering legal, professional advice. Since the details of your situation are fact dependent, you should additionally seek the services of a competent professional.

The opinions expressed by the author are not necessarily those of Tate Publishing, LLC.

Published by Tate Publishing & Enterprises, LLC
127 E. Trade Center Terrace | Mustang, Oklahoma 73064 USA
1.888.361.9473 | www.tatepublishing.com

Tate Publishing is committed to excellence in the publishing industry. The company reflects the philosophy established by the founders, based on Psalm 68:11,
"The Lord gave the word and great was the company of those who published it."

Book design copyright © 2016 by Tate Publishing, LLC. All rights reserved.
Cover design by Dante Rey Redido
Interior design by Richell Balansag

Published in the United States of America

ISBN: 978-1-68293-967-3
Religion / Christian Life / Personal Growth
16.03.23

This book is dedicated to my father:
Wilbur H. (Tommy) Thompson.
He never wavered, but always pressed on
to the Next Right Thing. You left your mark, Dad.

ACKNOWLEDGEMENTS

Physicians and attorneys call their business their "practice." I have often wished that the dilemmas and conundrums facing me as a pastor could be viewed as "practice" as well. That would give the urgency and size of life's questions a bit more leeway to be explored instead of requiring an instant answer. Truth be known, I have been practicing all my life. The congregations I have served have graciously, if unknowingly, granted me serial apprenticeships to practice spiritual triage and observe faith in practice.

I want to thank the willing and gracious recipients of my practice: the congregations of Bear Valley Church, Trinity Baptist Church, and Berean Baptist Church. You have watched my practice in preaching, teaching, pastoral care, and personal counsel. You have taught me more than I have taught you. You have followed my lead, gently corrected my blind spots, and filled in for my gaps. My life is a tapestry of memories of you. Your lives infuse the words of this book, and cascade through my memory as a priceless treasure.

My closest companion, my wife Joanne, recognizes most acutely the difference between the theologian and the practitioner. Without her grace and constant resilience to encourage the practice that is still imperfect, this life, nor this book, would have been possible.

CONTENTS

INTRODUCTION

The Worst-Case Scenario

His divine power has given us everything
we need for life and godliness...

—2 Peter 1:3

In the summer of 1981, a young pilot was attempting to cross over the Continental Divide west of Denver. His flight would take him just above the highway passing through the Eisenhower tunnel. But his Cessna 172 was flying too low and the crags of Colorado's Rocky Mountains were too high. His plane lacked the power to overcome a series of tactical errors that had created a pilot's worst nightmare.

Alone, with his pulse racing and his mind spinning, he had no good choices left. His panic and disbelief could not change the reality confronting him. He was seconds from death, about to slam into the unforgiving mountainside. Too little altitude. Too little power. Too many wrong decisions. No one to rescue him. What was he to do next?

It is one thing to know theory about handling a hard choice like this. It's another thing to apply the theory in practice, under pressure, at the instant it's needed.

What this young pilot did next was amazing. It was the next, and only, right thing. His decisive action, and the outcome, provides a rich metaphor to describe the importance of choosing the next right thing in any life crisis. His experience illustrates how a hard, even desperate, choice can literally save your life. By his choice and actions, he not only avoided disaster but he gained hope and confidence for the rest of his life.

This pilot walked away from his crisis without a scratch, but the choice he made was not an easy one for his ego or his wallet. His Cessna 172 ended up splayed across the mountainside like a hat-pinned moth in a biology display case. He chose to crash it there on purpose. Amazingly, the plane was fully intact with no visible damage. There it rested, an eye-catching curiosity for every traveler going eastbound on I-70, just above the west portal of the Eisenhower Tunnel.

As thousands of travelers saw his plane, an aluminum monument to the dangers of mountain flying and the presumptions of a young pilot, many onlookers shook their heads and passed judgment. However, for the young pilot who made the life-saving decision at eleven thousand feet, it was the brilliant choice to do the next right thing.

Hard choices:

Our imaginary, bump-free life is punctuated by real, hard choices that come at us in two general categories. One type is primarily self-imposed; the hard choices of opportunity. The buffet line of life sometimes offers too many options, and I carry too small a plate. Our culture serves up stress through an ever-expanding array of products, accessories, and opportunities. It's hard to choose. Which app, which movie, which menu item, which car, which house, and which college will best serve my needs and desires? The choices are not always this benign, but their sheer volume and complexity make for confusion and stress. This book is not about these kinds of choices, where the pressure mounts in futile attempts to squeeze too much opportunity into limited resources of time and energy.

This book is about an altogether different category of hard choices. These are the unwelcomed choices imposed by necessity. These hard choices do not allure our appetites; they threaten our very existence. Necessary choices arise when predicaments impinge on life without invitation and usually without warning. These choices do not sing with the alluring voice of opportunity. They reverberate with the strident warnings of impending crisis.

These choices are not complex but painfully simple. Something must be done now, or things will only get worse. But there are no easy solutions. These are hard choices precisely because they are stark, scary, recurring, and disappointing. There is no wiggle room, no array of options, and no escape ramps. They are forced upon us in circumstances we wouldn't naturally choose. We don't like this dilemma. We resist or resent being here at this stage of life. It isn't fair. But we can't see any magic solution, any fix-it trick, or a way to make everything all right. We have come face-to-face with a hard choice, a simple choice, a singular choice, and we don't like what we see.

The pages that follow address this kind of mess and how you can still choose to do the next right thing. The pressures and necessities that generate this kind of hard choice can take the form of:

- Unemployment
- Divorce

- Foreclosure
- Bankruptcy
- Betrayal
- Chronic or terminal illness
- Marital conflict
- A prodigal child
- Injury or accident
- Business failure
- Grief
- Injustice
- Racism
- Slander
- Aging parent

All of us at some point come face-to-face with a hard choice forced on us by necessity. If you know nothing but cafeteria-line stresses, candy store opportunities, and golden successes, you will no doubt dismiss this counsel as depressing, defeatist, and small-minded. But if you have firsthand experience with a dilemma similar to these listed here, you know about hard choices. You know the claustrophobia of having few options. You have felt the desperation as the walls press in. You are acquainted with the dull, gray waiting room. You have grieved and feared the narrowing of your shrinking autonomy. You have panicked at the prospect of an unknown future. You have cried out to God for help, for a sign, for some relief.

I've been there, and so have you. At times like this, there is no painless option. There is no other option than to make the call, to cut our losses, change plans, or start again.

Life is full of scenarios which require a hard choice, or a series of hard choices, just to hold the fort or manage the train wreck. Not one of them was planned or dreamed about. None of them set everything straight. And always the question is, is there any decision that is right in this situation? Is it right only if it's quick painless, or affordable? Is it right only if it's clever, simple and final? Is it wrong if it hurts or delays my goals? What is God's will? Does this hard situation prove that we have missed something, or blown it, or sped past some warning sign? Will there ever be joy and freedom again?

All these situations are hard. Their pain does not diminish by denial. They cannot be recast or managed by a new vision. They demand clear, simple, and hard choices. But what *is* the next right thing?

In the crush of such hard choices, it is easy to forget that God is still working. This is no mere platitude. He hasn't abandoned the planet. He hasn't forgotten us. He is not stumped by complex circumstances nor surprised by our attitude. He is not bereft of guidance. In fact, he has given counsel and made specific promises for just such predicaments as mine or yours.

One such promise from God that is easily dismissed or overly spiritualized in the crux of a hard choice is articulated by the Apostle Peter:

"His divine power has given us everything we need for life and godliness" (2 Pet. 1:3).

This is a promise that not only instructs us by principle but also energizes bold choices by the example of its author. The Apostle Peter is the writer, and his recipients are not tourists sifting through vacation brochures. They are pilgrims—he calls them aliens and strangers—who are pressured by ethnic tensions, political injustice, and economic hardship. They have put their faith in God, but all their choices are hard. Though oppressed and limited in resources, the apostle writes to them these words of universal application.

God has given us everything we need. Not everything we can dream up, nor everything someone else has. He gives me everything we need to remain vitally alive, and everything sufficient to display a faithful witness for Him. Even when life is hard, constricted, painful, disappointing, and dangerous, we have everything we need. Even here, at what seems the end of our tether, God has given us everything necessary.

Choosing the next right thing:

What might that "everything" be? It is "the next right thing." No matter what our dilemma, limitation, or fear, we are not beyond making the next choice the right choice, even if it's not pleasant. God promises, and Peter prescribes in the following verses, what that next right choice may be. It will be a handhold on reality that will enable us to not only hang on, but to ascend with greater confidence. These handholds have more to do with forming our character than with fixing our circumstances.

The next right thing will not mend everything that is broken. It is often the hard choice we didn't want to see. Sometimes it is the obvious option we had avoided or put off because of fear. It's the next right thing that may appear partial, inconclusive, or inadequate, but which ultimately results in renewed faith, greater effectiveness, and clearer purpose tomorrow.

Our choices may be few. Not one of them is attractive. No option promises peaceful closure. We may wonder if we have somehow slipped off God's radar or missed his perfect will. But He has us, and our hard choice, firmly in his grip. There is a response that is the next right thing. And if it's the right thing, it is from Him and promises a whole new purchase on the future. It's designed for now, this situation, and we can hold on to it with confidence.

At times like this we need perspective. When I first saw that small plane stranded above the tunnel portal, I cringed in vicarious embarrassment for that young pilot who crashed. What was he going to say to his friends or family? I wondered about the huge expense of dismantling and salvaging the plane. My perspective changed when I asked a pilot friend, "What went wrong?"

With dispassionate linear analysis, my pilot friend deconstructed the mishap into its component parts. "The pilot did almost everything wrong. He made a succession of bad decisions, starting with his flight plan, his experience level, and including his final approach to the mountain pass." This model of plane was marginal, at best, to safely clear this twelve-thousand-foot pass through the Rockies. The engine wasn't turbo-charged and needed ideal conditions to fly at this altitude. More telling, however, was the direction the pilot had been flying. Because small aircraft behave like cottonwood spores on the unseen currents of air and because near mountains wind sheer and downdrafts can be severe, an experienced pilot always allows for the potential of very sudden, strong winds. He will zigzag his way toward a high pass, flying almost parallel to the range, approaching the pass at a slight angle. That way, in the event of sudden loss of altitude, he can sheer off toward the valley, circle around, and try again. This pilot's biggest error was that he was flying directly at the pass, and when the plane was not high enough or he got caught in a sudden downdraft, there was no way to correct. He left no margin for error. It was a recipe for death.

"But I have to give this pilot credit," said my friend. "His very last decision was exactly right." It was the best of all the choices he had made that day and a decision to be admired even by veteran pilots. It took guts and skill. When he saw that he was certain to crash head-on into the mountainside, the pilot, at the last instant, pulled up on the stick, stalling the plane's forward airspeed, which caused it to flutter gently to the ground like a falling leaf on the porch. When his life was on the line, he did the one next right thing he could have done, and he walked away to fly another day, a much wiser pilot.

This pilot performed at his highest level by making a crucial, hard choice. In the crisis, he was not trying to achieve perfection nor even to reach his intended destination. He just wanted to avoid catastrophic loss. His options were reduced to one thing: just one next, and only, right thing. When everything, including his life, was on the line, he actually accomplished a resounding victory. He did the next right thing. He walked away, to pick up the pieces, and resume his life with new wisdom earned in the crucible of a crisis.

This is an essential survival strategy when life engulfs us. At such times, we don't feel heroic. We feel afraid, overmatched, and bereft of skill. We think in minutes, not months: the next breath, not health club workout routines.

Life gets compressed, and options narrow. It isn't just pilots strapped into thin-clad aluminum airplanes that experience this. Every one of us faces hard choices. And the question is, "What to do in this situation?" When not only my visible body, measurable livelihood, or treasured marriage is at risk but also my hopes, dreams, and assumptions are crushed, what is left? What good is a faith that doesn't keep me buoyant and aloft? How can I be a leader, or stay in the game, or sense any fellowship with God and others when a debacle is at my doorstep? When all the work, love, investment, or passion of a decade is put in peril by the next decision, how can I possibly do anything that is right, good, or godly?

In my experience, the next right thing is often the only tool available when drawn into the tangled and agonizing complexity of human dilemmas. Even as a pastor, mentor of men, and lifelong student of Scripture, the limits of human knowledge arise every day. There is no magical gymnastic move to counsel a couple out of overwhelming credit card debt. There are questions birthed in devastating loss which do not yield to bumper sticker answers. The frequently asked question "Why?" is impossible to answer. We don't know the future, so we journey together through dilemma-ridden lives.

Life at walking speed:

Instead of soaring in flight, the next right thing is done at walking speed. The apostle Peter and the faith heroes of the past were pedestrians. Though *pedestrian* is often used to imply dullness, ordinariness, and mediocrity, the Bible uses it as a simple description of faithful movement. We "walk" with God. We are to "walk" by faith. We are admonished to "walk" in the Spirit. When we live and walk this way, we are living moment by moment in dependence, relationship, and faith. And, we are progressing one step at a time, just one next right thing at a time. At this pace, we are practicing instantaneous obedience to wisdom with practical, incremental steps. We walk trustingly and humbly by lamplight, not by satellite imagery. When we walk in this way and choose the next right thing, we demonstrate that we are humble, teachable, alert, and available. We become satisfied to be pedestrians.

Fortunately, our path as Christ followers is well-trodden by men and women who simply walked, at pedestrian pace, as disciples. Their initial steps of faith became a reiterated march of obedience. They did what was next. They obeyed what was right. This book echoes with the faith journey of such people, primarily the example of Peter.

Sometimes we don't recognize these Bible heroes as peers or pedestrians like us. Scripture has compressed their lives into a few verses. We forget that we are seeing the video highlights, often on fast-forward. If we slow down to appreciate the sequences, the wide spans of time, and dwell on their real fears and tears, we will begin to recognize their earthy humanity. Then we will learn to imitate their walk and participate with them in the story of God in this present world. Their pace and choices will powerfully remind us that life is kept full by retaining and savoring the droplets of guidance, the increments of obedience, the flickers of light which came as they sequentially chose the next right thing. They walked. Nobody sprinted. That was all that was necessary.

For personal application:

1. What hard choices are you facing right now that have no easy solutions?

2. Is it reassuring or depressing to know that in some situations there is no perfect fix?

3. What are the fears that have kept your mind spinning and rendered you unable to make a decision?

4. What have you believed about God's concern for your problems that might not be true?

1

Welcome to Basecamp

Simon Peter, a servant and
apostle of Jesus Christ...

—2 Peter 1:1

The Climb Ahead: Welcome to basecamp. I will be your climbing coach. I'm here to teach you how to see, assess, and ascend what may look to be an impossible challenge. Be a learner. I will push you to your limits to develop your strength. Hone your skills. Climbing is a sport of agility, strength, and constant practice. It's also exhausting, painful, and dangerous. You will learn that climbing is equal parts skill and courage. It can be both beautiful and harrowing. You will advance only by making major commitments followed by thousands of micro decisions. I will teach you how to stay alive.

At every point of any climb, you will be dependent on handholds. Then, just as you have found a secure one, you must immediately start looking for the next one. Your grip, your vision, your courage, and your strength will be tested repeatedly as you ascend. Master these handholds and become adept at employing them. Your progress and your very life will hang on them as you tackle the challenges that loom above you.

My full name is Simon Peter. I want you to know me by this name. It's more than two random proper nouns. My name is a capsule summary of my whole identity and my climbing résumé. It's the branding on my life, my accomplishments, and my reputation. I use it, say it, and sign it, knowing that it represents everything I've done and all I've promised. It's axiomatic that no one can claim to really know me, or trust my counsel, without knowing my name.

Furthermore, my name will mean little to you unless you know something of my history. Therefore, please know me by my name and what that name represents. I've been climbing for a long time, and I've signed this name into many a summit registry. I am an active practitioner of the very things I want to pass along to you. Neither you nor I will ever outgrow our need for these handholds. Join me for the climb of your life.

El Capitan is a vertical rock formation in Yosemite National Park on the north side of Yosemite Valley, near its western end. This granite monolith looms three thousand feet over the valley floor and is the largest slab of smooth granite on the planet. It has proved an irresistible challenge for rock climbers over the last half century.

In January 2015, Tommy Caldwell and Kevin Jorgeson spent nineteen days completing what *Rock and Ice Magazine* called the "hardest climb of all time." They free-climbed the seemingly unclimbable Dawn Wall of El Capitan in thirty-two pitches of relentless, scary, finger-shredding doggedness.

Caldwell had studied the wall for seven years, wondering if it could ever be free-climbed. In the jargon-rich environment of climbing, this term needs definition. *Free-climbing* does not mean climbing without ropes or protection. It does not imply scampering from bottom to top in one continuous ascent. *Free-climbing* is climbing without supporting oneself artificially on ropes, bolts, or pitons. Yes, protection is utilized, but each pitch, or section, must be climbed using only the natural footholds and handholds. No "hangdogging" (hanging from the rope while ascending a hard route). Caldwell and Jorgeson climbed each section using only the tiniest edges and slivers of rock as their means of ascent. They fell countless times trying to free-climb each pitch in its purest form. Only when they had each climbed it without aid did they advance to the next pitch.

Looking at pictures or watching videos of this duo is breathtaking. The footholds and handholds are credit-card thin. The exposure is paralyzing. They spent the majority of their climb tackling blank faces of crack-free granite, ascending a vertical route that is barely there, discernable only to the eye of the undaunted.

It took incredible vision and determination to accomplish this unprecedented climb. But it also required tenacious skill and raw athletic strength. When the Dawn Wall is first encountered, it seems impossible. No one could climb such a featureless, threatening, vertical face. But pitch by pitch, through careful examination, Tommy Caldwell discovered that there were, in fact, tiny handholds that could render the route climbable. He reduced the climb to increments and proceeded to grasp one tiny flake of granite at a time to advance toward the summit. Move by move, section by section, the climb advanced. What was initially paralyzing in aggregate became possible in increments. Tommy Caldwell and Kevin Jorgeson simply did the next right thing thousands of times until the summit was reached.

Nothing is insurmountable:

Our personal El Capitans loom over us with similar insurmountability. They appear unclimbable. But these personal and spiritual challenges can be tackled in the same manner as the Dawn Wall climb. This is not to bleach our world of the miraculous by ceasing to pray for divine intervention. Nor is this an encouragement to practice a religion of self-reliance. Rather, we simply need to acknowledge that most of the time, we are not borne aloft on wings. We need to climb. And we can climb. Our challenge is to see and grip the handholds available this moment and ascend by the increments that God is showing us.

People like us, meaning people who know trouble, affliction, and failure, are often overwhelmed by the foreboding vertical wall of impossibility before us. This is when we need a coach, an encourager, a mentor. We need a climbing partner who has faced similar obstacles and overcome them. We need someone to break down the massiveness of our trouble into doable steps and handholds. Just when the rock seems unscalable, we are introduced to the coach named Peter. In his school, we will learn to climb. We will watch him climb. He will teach us handholds that will arm us with an array of climbing skills for any terrain in life. He has written a curriculum for any willing climber. But first let's get to know the man.

Peter comes to us through his writing, the "letter from Peter," archived in the New Testament. The first two words of this letter are his name: "Simon Peter." They summarize his amazing biography in microcosm. He could have chosen to be known by one name or the other, but he chooses this compound form, and for a reason. An incredible life lies behind this dual name and the brief letter he writes. Knowing the epic biography behind this name infuses every word of this compact instruction with Peter's own personal experience. If we read between the lines, we will

made a commitment or showed any courage to compete. What a squandered opportunity. I'm sick and disappointed. What a dream killer you are, Alan Webb!

It's the same sickening desperation I get as I watch the mishandling of opportunity by the raw, talented disciple named Simon Peter. At times we can't figure out which identity he is living. Simon, who breathed the same air and walked the same miles as the Son of Man, is exhibit "A" for displaying that advantage does not always translate into diligence, nor privilege into success. Simon had raw strength, talent, and a big personality. He gave a great press conference, proved to be a natural leader, and was gung ho to please. But Simon also had so many moments of spectacular loopiness, transparent hubris, and ghastly betrayal. What an accident waiting to happen! What a team wrecker and poster boy for disappointment for everyone else and especially for himself. His early career was marked by overpromise and under delivery. He wasn't incorrigible, but neither did he seem especially bright. So often he just didn't get it. No single individual needed correction and rebuke by Jesus, both privately and publicly, as frequently as this walking contradiction, Simon Peter.

Nevertheless, say what you will about him; he held nothing back. He publicly stepped forward to pledge loyalty to his Master. He alone left the security of the boat to risk walking on water, and he stood single-handedly to defend Jesus with a borrowed sword. Simon often paid the price for his visible, sometimes brash, spontaneity. His buoyant suggestion to consummate the transfiguration with an exclusive campout including himself, Jesus, and Elijah was strongly rejected by Jesus as contrary to the Lord's own purposes. He was roundly rebuked by Jesus (immediately after receiving his new name and identity as Peter, the rock) for his resistance to God's will that Jesus would surrender his life and die on the cross. Jesus even categorized Peter's repugnance to the cross as inspired by Satan himself (Matt. 16:23). He was repeatedly embarrassed and disheveled by his own outbursts of human fallibility. At times everyone around Peter must have groaned and wondered, "What are you doing? What were you thinking? Wake up! You're blowing your opportunity! Keep your mouth shut, Peter! Run to the level of your potential!"

Simon Peter is a handful, a complex personality, a high-maintenance disciple. Along with his incredible courage and his unvarnished love and loyalty, Peter displayed more than his allotted quotient of foolishness. He was impetuous and boastful. At several critical moments, he was asleep, quite literally. This raw follower was an inscrutable amalgam of competitiveness, impetuosity, and disloyalty.

Jesus isn't finished:

The most notorious of all Peter's failings is well-known and documented by the apostle John (John 18–20). Peter openly swore loyalty to Jesus, even if it meant standing all alone to the death. But the next thing we know, he is denying any association with Jesus, swearing with oaths that he doesn't even know him—cowering under a simple question from a harmless servant girl. Peter flees and hides, but skulks back to witness his Master in the throes of death. In a poignant moment, Jesus, in the breathless agony of his own suffering on the cross, looks piercingly at Peter, bringing crushing conviction and causing him to weep bitterly in regret.

If we left the story there, Peter would be a biblical Alan Webb at his Olympic trials debacle. Peter would have been reduced again to the rawboned and tragic Simon. His legacy would have been that of a highly privileged, deeply flawed, and desperately disappointing draft choice. It's all the more amazing, then, that after his resurrection, Jesus came looking specifically for Peter. In the end, Jesus singled out this man, Simon Peter, with all his amassed record of failure, for tender and merciful restoration.

The poignant encounter is recorded in John 21. Jesus calls him by his family name, Simon. He summons Simon's love and challenges him with a life-defining assignment. This is how Simon again received and experienced grace when he needed it most. Simon came to see that he was not just the sum total of his failings, nor the projection of his most dismal performance on his worst day. He was forgiven and transformed by his Master, not on the podium of victory but down under the bleachers, where he was hiding in lonely defeat. Jesus came after him in his disgrace, embraced him when he still stunk, and called to him when he wished he could just crawl away and die, or hide forever in his shame. This relentless grace was the beginning of the end for the old Simon and the birth of the new man Peter.

There is some dark and inscrutable psychology in many of our heroes that seems set on subverting their own success. It is true for today's heroes and for many we observe in the Bible. Many seem to tragically, even masochistically, snatch defeat from the jaws of victory. This moth-to-the-flame self-destruction is maddening, even horrifying, to witness, and very sad. It's scary and fascinating all at once. But perhaps we are drawn to these flawed characters because we more easily hear rumbling echoes and see dark vestiges of ourselves in them. We crave their talent and success, but we viscerally identify with their flaws. They seem so human, so like us. We have the same capacity to blow the opportunity, blurt the wrong words, or abandon our post in fear. We want to be Peter, but we identify with Simon. We want Peter's precious faith, but it often seems unattainable because we know we harbor the weaknesses of Simon.

This is why knowing something of the journey of how Simon became Peter is as instructive as reading his wise words. It's also encouraging because of the countless failures in my own life.

Simon's very first encounter with Jesus displays the paradox he was. Luke 5:1–11 records how Jesus was standing on the shore of the Sea of Galilee, teaching the people. Seeing two boats and their owners nearby, Jesus asked to be launched out from the shore so that he could teach the people from the boat. In one of the most familiar stories of Scripture, when he is done teaching, Jesus challenges Simon to "put out into deep water, and let down your nets for a catch." Already weary from a fishless all-nighter, Simon resists but summons minimal energy to placate the Master with compliance. Then came that storied catch so large they had to call for help to save their nets from breaking. The bounty was so huge it almost sank both boats. What a sign. What an indisputable demonstration of divine power and grace.

It was at this point that Simon displayed something at once incisively prophetic and sadly pathetic. This proved to be a harbinger of his early apostolic experience. He shows what so many of us know of ourselves: devotion and dysfunction, all twisted into a shapeless wad of neediness. He fell at Jesus's feet in an act of unrehearsed and unselfconscious worship. Peter was instantly humbled, intensely grateful, and smitten. In pure transparency, he cried, "Go away from me, Lord; I am a sinful man."

This first response when he found himself at ground level with divine power and holiness was exactly right. He was slain in fear and awe. He worshiped. Simon was laid bare, undefended, and indefensible. He was instantly stripped of all self-confidence and grasped that he could not live in the white-hot intensity of Jesus's holiness and majesty. He knew at once the might, purity, and overpowering-ness of the Lord's awesome authority. He had fallen into the hands of the living God, utterly condemnable in his sin. His abjectly humble response to holiness was exactly right.

But then Simon resorted to his native instincts. With reflexive, terrified urgency, he just wanted to get away to safety, to dodge the laser beam aimed at his iniquity. He blurted, "Go away from me, Lord; I am a sinful man!" All he can think about is how to get away, to preserve himself from the incinerating fire of Jesus's power and holiness. Simon didn't completely grasp the rest of the transaction that Jesus had in mind. He didn't seem to hear Jesus's invitation not only to worship in awe but to stay in relationship. Even as Simon reflexively wants to get away, Jesus wants Peter to draw closer and take on a new way of life. Jesus is opening the door to Simon to be transformed into a new identity, to become a new man.

Simon is being introduced to grace, but he doesn't quite absorb it the first time around. At just that moment, when Simon is completely undone, lost, abjectly repentant, and flailing, Jesus spoke, "Don't be afraid." And in a brief sentence, Jesus shows Simon his redeemed future and his new assignment in life: "From now on you will catch men." From complete spiritual asphyxiation, Simon's lungs are instantly filled with life-giving grace. He is miraculously and undeservedly made alive again. He is reborn. Immediately,

Simon displays what becomes his signature: wholehearted, unreserved, instantaneous, and obedient action. He leaves everything and follows Jesus. From that instant, the fisherman became a disciple, an initiator, a spokesman. The muscle used for pulling on oars and halyards is transformed into courage for leadership. His powerful grip for working the rigging of a fishing boat was applied to a singular loyalty for his rabbi. His eagerness and transparency were everything a teacher could want in a disciple.

But this transformation was not instantaneous. There was still a bumpy ride ahead for Jesus, for the twelve, and for Simon on his way to becoming Peter. This is the man who writes his full name as the signature at the top of his letter, a name full of irony and paradox, but also, strength and hope.

I am Simon:

It's the Simon in me that is drawn toward the miracle of this transformation. It's the Simon in me that is fascinated with the messiness of his sanctification. It's the Simon in me that yells at Alan Webb blowing the race, or Simon denying the Lord, because I recognize myself in him. It's classic transference. He is me, fumbling the opportunity and underperforming when the going gets tough. Simon is the man in me that reneges from the challenge, shrinks in fear, and dissembles under pressure. Simon is the puny man, the caricature within. I live with Simon, but I want to be Peter. I long to unite the bifurcated person within me, to become as fruitful and faithful as the Simon Peter who writes his letter. I crave to see the transformative power of Jesus become more than theological theory, especially in my own life. I want to be whole, as Simon Peter became whole, a fully integrated person bearing the descriptors "servant" and "apostle" comfortably and unselfconsciously.

Fortunately, the legacy of Simon Peter is not restricted to the narrative of his early apostolic life, as inspiring as that is. In God's providence, and with the Holy Spirit's inspiration, we also have his words of counsel and instruction that come after a lifetime of being battle tested. He can serve as a coach with the distilled wisdom of firsthand experience. In the space of a few verses, we can receive the life-defining vision for our own transformation. It begins with God, who has given us everything we need, but it is matched by spiritual handholds for our ascent into maturity. One-by-one, they will call us to wise and godly responses to the troubles of our day and the trials of our lives. Listen to the living voice of this fully integrated disciple, Simon Peter, as he speaks to the challenges you face today. He will show you the next right thing.

For personal application:

1. Have you observed someone who scaled a seemingly unclimbable mountain? What was it, and how did they do it?

2. Which part of Simon Peter do you most identify with? Why?

3. Is there unused or misused potential in you? Have you given up, like Simon?

4. If God told you who you are and what you are called to do, would you believe Him?

2

Trust Is Everything

Simon Peter, a servant and apostle of Jesus
Christ, to those who through the righteousness
of our God and Savior Jesus Christ have
received a faith as precious as ours.

—2 Peter 1:1

Handhold #1: Faith

Lesson number one: when your life depends on it, you had better be anchored to something that doesn't move. Every climber knows this, but sometimes we are fooled by appearances. In the summer of 1988, Paul Piana and Todd Skinner almost lost their lives when their anchor moved. They were just topping out on the route known as the Salathé on El Capitan. It had taken six grueling weeks to score this triumph, and they were finishing the very last pitch, three thousand feet above the valley floor. Paul had wrapped a sling around a seemingly secure seven-foot-tall slab of granite. Almost as an afterthought, he clipped an extra rope to an old piton driven into a nearby seam. As his partner ascended to join him in victory at the top, to their horror, the giant block broke loose and started to roll off the ledge with Paul and Todd tied to it.

Todd was struck by the massive rock, breaking several ribs and severing his rope. Paul's leg was broken in five places as the boulder rolled over his left side. In that horrifying instant, they both thought they were plunging to their deaths. But a split-second later, they were arrested by the second rope. That second line, clipped into that old piton, had saved them both. It was driven into immovable solid rock, and it held. Lesson learned.

"My life has had many changes. Jana and I are separated. Our marriage will end sometime this spring. I am sad about that, but I feel I did what I could to prevent this. Her persistent unwillingness to hear me and compromise brought me to this end. She said she wanted it to work and even agreed the ball was largely in her court. But she didn't do the work necessary to back up those words.

I was fired last September for no good reason other than greed. It was a "good Christian man" who did the deed. You may anticipate my next comment: my faith is gone. I can't count on God. My prayers have all come back COD. I know God is still there, but he has a plan that I don't understand. And I can't see myself in that plan."

So writes a friend about his "faith." I have files full of counseling notes and e-mails that document a similar route to the cul-de-sac where faith lurches to a stop. Faith, it seems, is anything but solid. Faith has become one of the most elastic words in our popular culture. Though frequently cited, it is seldom defined and even more rarely anchored. Though soaring and inspirational, its wings often seem to melt in the heat like candle wax, and its daring heroes plummet haplessly to the ground.

We hear stories of faith on prime-time TV. A star athlete recalling his dark days of injury, surgery, and rehabilitation speaks to reporters about his resilience: "I relied on my faith to get me through those hard days." Cancer survivors, flood victims, and parents of special needs children speak into the interviewer's microphone: "My faith gives me strength through the dark times."

When I hear this kind of testimony, I experience a profound ambivalence. On the one hand, I'm inspired. The fact that a person uses the term *my faith* reveals something intensely personal and meaningful. I rejoice to hear of a vibrant inner life that is deeper than the speaker's current circumstances. After all, faith is meant to be that invisible source of inner strength. It's our most intimate expression of trust in God.

On the other hand, I can't squelch an insistent question in my mind: "Your faith in what...your faith in whom?" A curiosity, even skepticism, arises with the use of the phrase *my faith*. Too often, I fear, it expresses a faith that is tied to nothing more than unanchored bits and pieces of positive thinking, Yankee ingenuity, and good luck mantras.

Does my faith hold?

A real question for me, for you, for all strugglers in crisis is this: is *my faith* merely happy thoughts hanging on skyhooks of optimism and now confirmed because I had a positive outcome? Is *my faith* supported only by gossamer cobwebs of religious nostalgia or a boutique collection of motivational slogans? Or is *my faith* anchored in *the* faith in God who is revealed, objective, and personal?

Everything Peter has to say to people facing hard choices depends on his starting point: faith. Where does it start, and what holds it fast? What does it mean to have faith, especially when the going gets tough? Over my years of pastoring, I can't count the number of people I have counseled and tried to comfort in crises of faith. Their wounds and woes include almost every form of mishap, disease, betrayal, and injustice imaginable in a fallen world. The agonies include scenarios like the following:

Kris and Teri's wedding featured a carriage pulled by white stallions and a reception with Wolfgang Puck cuisine. Bride and groom soared off to a Polynesian honeymoon. But now they sit in isolated, untouching bitterness. A vacuous silence has replaced what was once a romantic and gauzy dream. That dream is dying, wilting under an acid rain of unforgiveness that drizzles on a once verdant promise. Like a termite-riven house of wood, they are held together only by the thinnest coat of paint on the outside. The original fiber of a covenant has been eaten away by the craven nibblings of a thousand faultfindings and a zillion put-downs. Can either of them still have faith or do anything right in this infested environment?

Scott's promising, bold, and creative business plan now lies drowning in a pool of red ink. With brilliant insight, he had detected the niche for business profit and had foreseen the market potential. But the economy hit a downdraft, potential customers halted their investment, and his beautiful, intrepid strategy is brushed aside like a weightless leaf, as fragile and vulnerable as the wisp of thought from which it was created. The dream crashes, and along with it, the lien is called, the house foreclosed, and a family is left floundering in breathless panic, its leader a broken arrow. What does Scott's faith have to offer now? What is the next right thing for Scott and his wife?

John and Sarah awaited the birth of their first child with tip-toe eagerness. The nursery is fully prepared and state-of-the-art. It is festooned with wallpaper borders, a glider rocker, baby toys, and lotions for every body part. A stroller designed like a Mercedes-Benz sits in the living room, ready for deployment. Diapers, changing table, socks the size of glove fingers, all perfectly color coordinated and monogrammed, await the arrival of this most wanted child. Then, at 3:00 a.m. during week twenty-seven, contractions begin. The baby is coming, on his own terms, and this gate-crashing entrance will render all these preparations instantly irrelevant. His lungs aren't functioning. His heart is weak, and it's uncertain whether his eyes will ever see the beauty of the colorful nursery designed for him. A normal, bouncing, and tender infancy has become an ongoing medical emergency. Everything is on hold. Incubators replace a mother's arms. Intubation, oxygen, monitors, and IVs entangle this three-pound patient and frustrate a father's desire to touch flesh, the skin of his firstborn. An army of specialists and an encyclopedic data dump overwhelm these fledgling parents and their innate desire to hold and cuddle a normal infant. What can John and Sarah believe in that will carry them through this crisis? What can they choose at this point that could possibly give them the vitality and Christlikeness promised by Peter?

John the Baptist was there. His faith was sorely tested, and wavering. Of all the endorsements on one's résumé, John had the best. Jesus himself said, "Truly I say to you, among those born of women there has arisen no one greater than John the Baptist" (Matt. 11:11). Look at John's life. He performed a prenatal leap for joy in his mother's womb when he heard Mary's voice; he was the first to announce the Messiah to Israel. He baptized Jesus and saw the Holy Spirit descend on him like a dove. John is famous for his faith-inspired humility when his ministry was being eclipsed by the burgeoning ranks of Jesus's followers: "He must become greater; I must become less" (John 3:26, 30).

But John's faith ran aground. He couldn't sustain it with sheer grittiness and guts. He was thrown into prison for confronting power with piercing truth, and it must have seemed an ignominious fate for a prophetic forerunner. It wasn't his lack of creature comforts that made him doubt. He was made for austerity and hardness. But he must have thought: *I'm family. I've believed all along. I've faithfully proclaimed the message. So where is the promised liberation, the messianic authority?* Jesus didn't break down the walls or send an earthquake to fling open the jail cell. John's anchor seemed to be slipping. His faith wasn't working the way he thought it should.

John's faith floundered on one central question. "Are you the one who is to come, or shall we look for another?" (Matt. 11:2). Even though John knew Jesus came as a sacrificial Lamb and not a militaristic liberator, even though he knew that Jesus' central battle was against sin and not the Romans, his disappointments left him bereft of faith like a surprise uppercut knocks the wind out of a fighter. His doubts were as deep as it gets. *Have I believed and followed the wrong one all along? Nothing about this outcome assures me that I have vested trust in the right place.*

John's faith, as great as it was, was exposed for its Achilles heel. It was vulnerable to unforeseen circumstance, loneliness, and fear. Even a hero like John discovers the drain at the bottom of "my faith" and finds himself empty.

What Jesus does to restore solid faith is twofold. First, he reminds John of the irrefutable signs of his messiahship that John has witnessed for himself: the blind see, the lame walk, and even the dead are raised up. But then he takes John to the deepest foundation of faith that is even more substantial than all the miracles and evidences. He said, "Blessed is the one who is not offended by me" (Matt. 11:6). Many a person, like John, has earthly, political, personal, or healing expectations of Jesus. Our hope and our faith get anchored in the outcomes we so desire. We want him to run to our fire alarm, cure our diseases, or defeat the villains. On our schedule. According to our outrage. Because of our devotion. Now!

Jesus draws John to the bedrock of faith. "It's me," he says. "It's my person, my work, and my glory that you are to have at the core of your trust." Don't be offended when the seemingly obvious miracle isn't delivered but is supplanted by an even greater one. Jesus focuses faith on one object, himself, not a myriad of potential outcomes. Faith rests in Jesus, the Rock, and all he is and does, not just the swift resolution of this current crisis.

Precious faith:

This is where Peter picks up the subject of faith. "Precious faith" is how Peter summarizes his trust in the very first verse of his letter (2 Pet. 1:1). It summarizes God's grace experienced personally. This all-encompassing description of Peter's gratitude fills in the silent years since Jesus's restoration of his failed disciple and the writing of this letter. Peter opens a window, through this intimate and tender description, to his personal journey and his spiritual transformation. He is the only writer in the New Testament

47

to use this word translated "precious," and with it, he explains a relationship with his Master that has captured and revolutionized his life.

Faith is the very first handhold. Peter will describe and encourage the use of eight of these handholds, which will help us retain a grip on "life and godliness" (2 Pet. 1:3). They are urged on us as continuous and practical skills for effective and fruitful discipleship. All of them are trustworthy components. But all of them begin with this "precious faith." Peter lists them in a sequence that can be read in seconds but remains relevant for a lifetime (2 Pet. 1:5–8). "Faith" is where Peter begins.

"To those who through the righteousness of our God and Savior Jesus Christ have received a faith as precious as ours" (2 Pet. 1:2).

Peter, the manly man, is the only New Testament writer to use the word *precious*. He uses it twice, once in each of his letters (1 Pet. 1:19 and 2 Pet. 1:2). Here, he uses it to describe the faith he has received. It is faith anchored in the Person who sought him, washed him clean, and trained him up. This faith is precious because it isn't invented or fantasized by human longings. Peter wasn't looking for Jesus, but Jesus came looking and calling for him. Jesus drew Peter into faith, based on his demonstrations of miraculous power, authority, knowledge, and holiness. This faith is grounded in the Man, the Son of Man, the man of all men: Jesus, his Savior whom he knows and follows. This faith is a treasury of shared history, eye-witnessed miracles, and personal transformation.

This is a faith Peter holds onto with a fisherman's calloused grip. Faith in Jesus has produced a life-sustaining relationship that has grown richer through sorrow and joy, freedom and imprisonment. This faith is a source of continuous soul nourishment. Peter knows his faith is anchored in God and in His incarnate Son (John 5:24; Rom. 5:6–8). It is an objective faith, grounded in experienced fact, not mere subjective longing for things imagined. He has received this faith through the righteous life, atoning death, and propitiatory peace with God purchased on the cross by his Savior (1 John 5:11–13).

This is a faith that is completely distinct from feel-good, mystical fantasies, slavish idol worship, control freak perfectionism, or vague beliefs about innate human nobility. No. Jesus found Peter and called him to follow a real person with understandable words, practicing authentic godliness in the real world. It was God's initiative, the Savior's voice, and Peter's simple, trusting responses that he now describes as this "precious faith."

The faith of which Peter speaks was not muscled up because of his exasperated groping for meaning in life. It didn't arise from nebulous longings for connection with the supernatural. Instead, Peter put his faith in the righteous obedience of Jesus Christ (v 1), foreordained by God, and demonstrated on the cross. The Savior found Peter, and called Peter. By faith, Peter finally, and fully, received him. Peter found stability, not by questing, but by receiving. His faith was anchored in God, not in the attributes of his own fickle heart.

Conversely, when faith's anchor is merely subjective, it proves unstable. Everything in life seems suddenly in jeopardy. When the anchor point we thought was immovable begins to slide, we grasp for answers. Where is God? Why doesn't He show Himself? What have I done to deserve this? These questions are hurled into the abyss that swallows up our hopes and dreams. This kind of faith doesn't prove to be precious. It seems to be a cruel joke or a tragic mistake.

At such times of threat and suffering, it is natural to flail and to grasp at anything that will arrest the fall. At such times, these sufferers come seeking a listening ear, and they often want answers, guidance, and direction. Frequently, however, a more fundamental spiritual issue has tripped them up and has halted their progress toward wholeness. They are experiencing deep doubts about their faith and wonder if they even have faith anymore. They say with honesty and a quavering voice, "I guess my faith is just not strong enough. I don't know if I can really believe in God anymore."

Their faith has failed them. The bargain with God has not worked out, and they feel cheated by their investment in faith. Deep and scary questions threaten what once appeared settled and stable. What philosophers and theologians call the problem of evil has become very personal and has left them without a suitable answer to their pain. They ask questions like "Why has such a bad thing happened to a person like me? Why didn't prayer protect us from the tornado? Where's the promise that a Christian upbringing would inoculate my child from drug abuse? Why didn't giving to missions and tithing insulate my business from financial meltdown? After all that Bible study, why wasn't my marriage saved?" This crisis of faith will not be solved by a new formula. Some deeper theological thinking, coupled with a redesigned set of biblical assumptions, needs to shine light on their bruised faith.[1]

However, there's an even more systemic threat to faith than this—a threat that halts all progress and growth by promoting an endless and fruitless introspection regarding the genuineness of *my faith*.

My friend Jason repeatedly trips over his own feet on the starting line of faith. He has suffered many setbacks, losses, and disappointments. He is a believer and gamely tries to move forward as a disciple, but substantive change eludes him. Periodically, he attempts to implement the next right thing but always seems to get sidelined early in the process because he doubts his faith. It's not because he disbelieves the practical and personal wisdom of Peter's counsel. He doesn't grapple with the problem of evil. He can't seem to get a grip on the next right thing because he keeps circling back to reassess the first thing, the foundation of his faith. He keeps asking, "Am I really a Christian?" After several decades, he still wonders if he truly has faith. When trouble persists, he defaults to persistent doubt about his own salvation. He can't get past the starting line.

When I ask him why he has doubts, he takes me back to his first moments of faith, his experience of salvation. "I heard the Gospel message of salvation and went forward at the invitation to receive Christ as my Savior. I prayed the prayer. But now I don't know if I was sincere enough, whether I really confessed all my sin. I don't know if I really gave all my life to Jesus on that night, and I just wonder if all my fumbles and struggles with hard choices are a result of not having a real faith in Jesus Christ."

Jason's spiritual walk resembles a gerbil on his running wheel. It's sad and unnecessary. He makes no progress because he is constantly circling back to the starting point. His faith is just that: his. It is not the faith Peter proclaims that is based on God's call and Christ's righteousness (2 Pet. 1:2).

ROGER THOMPSON

This totally subjective examination of faith is debilitating.
Jason's "faith" is not an expansive journey with God but a
solitary confinement with his doubts. When faith represents
only subjective experience, it will always be lacking in
assurance. Jason dithers at the starting line, unable to
sustain the race, because when he looks for assurance of his
faith he replays the same old video, starring himself. Jason,
sadly, looks for assurance in a ritual ("I prayed the prayer")
or in his sincerity of the moment ("Did I give all of my life
to Jesus on that night?").

Peter's counsel to Jason would be, "Don't look for the
foundations of your faith by weighing your sincerity or
measuring your level of devotion on that night long ago."
Rather, ask yourself, "In whom do I believe? In whom have
I put my whole-soul trust?" Romans 10:9–10 is one of the
great compressed definitions of the saving faith: "That if
you confess with your mouth, 'Jesus is Lord'. and believe
in your heart that God raised him from the dead, you will
be saved. For it is with your heart that you believe and are
justified, and it is with your mouth that you confess and are
saved." This establishes faith as a present-tense assurance. It
is clear where this faith is placed, and in whom it is placed.
Confessing with your mouth "Jesus is Lord" and believing
the foundational truth of the Gospel that "God raised
him from the dead" give confidence and produce undying
gratitude. True New Testament faith is placing trust in the
objective truth of Christ's redeeming work.

Peter instructs us like a climbing instructor teaching pupils
whose lives will depend on their mastery of reliable, repeatable,
and ever-adaptable handholds. These are handholds he has
learned during years of clinging to Jesus. They will aid his
pupils, not only for survival but toward maturity and mastery
as they progress in their discipleship. And faith comes first.

Two big realities:

Peter learned to cling to Jesus in his life of faith as he became a walking work in progress. We can trace in his life, and even in his name, Simon Peter, the two biggest realities of the Christian life. Peter is the name that symbolizes justification, his new identity in Christ. In Simon, we can trace the progress toward Christ-likeness called sanctification.

Peter is the name that signifies the man who has been given, and receives, everything. He is justified by faith in Jesus Christ. He is the recipient of grace through faith. The instantaneous, once-for-all, trusting of the Son's finished work on the cross is the substance and ground of Peter's saving faith. He is forever repositioned in God's sight. He has crossed over from death to life, from darkness to light, from enemy to friend (John 5:24). His sin is covered, paid in full. Peter's faith is anchored in the objective accomplishment of Father and Son to kill death and remove its pall of fear over humankind. Once an alien and enemy because of an unpayable debt of sin, Peter is now justified by the mercies of God in the substitutionary sacrifice that paid all sin debt. His position is entirely, and irreversibly, changed.

That's the Peter we see in his humility, recognizing his bankrupt unholiness, and crying out, "Go away from me, Lord; I am a sinful man." It is the only response Peter, or any person, can make when pure holiness convicts the conscience. He repents in helplessness. But the Savior has a rescue Peter never could have imagined. Instead of abandoning this wretched man, he heals and restores him. Such unfathomable grace, displayed in purpose and power, is what changed Peter. Peter cast his empty-handed faith onto God's accomplished plan. He was saved. He was declared righteous. He was justified before God

But Simon still lurked in the shadows. His daily life did not immediately match the truth and freedom of his salvation. Simon the selfish. Simon the competitor. Simon the fearful and flaky. Simon the course and crude. Simon the braggart and traitor. Simon was not sin-free, or even sin-averse, as snapshots of him in the New Testament clearly display. Simon is the grim and surly shadow trailing the free and forgiven Peter. Simon is the old-natured fool sabotaging the new-natured apostle. Perhaps to many of us, as miraculous as is the justification of the condemnable sinner named Peter, even more stupendous is the sanctification of the renegade Simon. But this too is what the doubly named Simon Peter packed into this word *precious*.

The scent of sanctification wafts through these introductory words, and they bring hope to every struggling disciple. Now Peter turns into a coach. Whereas justification is anchored in what God has accomplished *for* us, sanctification is experienced by allowing God to work *in* and *through* us. We can't add anything to our position in Christ. We are justified solely by God's grace, plus nothing. But Peter insists that having been "given everything we need for life and godliness" (1:3), we now must "make every effort" (1:5) to participate in our calling and obedience. This is practical, daily, joyful obedience to a process theologians call "progressive sanctification." Simon Peter did not arrive at maturity by some magical transmigration. He learned his way into maturity by practicing his daily grip on handholds of practical spirituality.

This, too, began with Jesus and not in some kind of self-help makeover strategy. John records Peter's being summoned, challenged, and restored by Jesus (John 21:15–19.) Jesus calls for him specifically, calling him from the squalor of his ghastly performance and his pungent shame. What surprises and encourages me is that Jesus specifically and repetitively speaks to *Simon*, not Peter. Simon, not the Rock. Simon, the denier and oath spitter. Simon the turncoat. Simon the true but dysfunctional worshiper. Jesus calls to him and asks him essentially the same question three times: "Simon, do you truly love me?" Jesus uses his prefaith name, his pre-Rock identity with which to address him. It is Simon the failure he calls, forgives, and restores. It is in the old-person Simon that grace will show its transforming power. Simon is refitted and redeployed. Simon is shown his future with its sobering challenges. Simon is again called: "Follow me." Simon has a new life.

Remember the unpolished Simon's first response to Jesus? It contained sparkling clarity about his guilt: "I am a sinful man." This is conviction of the Holy Spirit. This is exactly, surgically correct. Only justification by grace at Christ's expense, received through faith, could save him. But Simon seems to make the same mistake many of us make. He embraced his new position but accepted his old identity. His faith at first did not change his definition of himself. He assumed his strengths and weaknesses were already set and unchangeable. Peter is the changed person, but Simon—well, he's unchangeably and irrevocably Simon. Did his reply become a self-fulfilling subscript, a subverting message that went something like this: "I am nothing more and will never be anything more than a sinful man."

Could it be that my experience mirrors Simon's? Though I have found freedom, forgiveness, and joy in salvation that Jesus freely offers, it isn't yet "precious." It's only for a part of me, the future, positional, and theological Peter. But the original Simon-in-the-flesh part of me is untouchably substandard. I'm still the old, unredeemable, pathetic Simon. I am a sinful man. I'm a box of worthless flesh and unworthiness, but I have a faith that one day I will be delivered to my home in heaven. Once my sad transit through this world is done, I'll "have a new name written down in glory." But on earth, I'm just a sinner saved by grace.

Jesus called all of Simon Peter. That's why his faith is precious. By the power of a threefold appeal, Jesus pulls Simon over an unforgettable threshold (John 21:15–19): "Do you love me?" Jesus asks three times. "Yes, Lord, you know I love you," Simon answers, three times. "Feed my lambs, take care of my sheep, feed my sheep," is Jesus's triple repetition and call. And then, finally, Jesus simply says what he did at the lakeside, calling to the husky fisherman, so eager and raw: "Follow me." Jesus wants Simon, yes, Simon, to hear his call into service and usefulness, after all he has fumbled and mishandled. Simon, you are not a loser. "Sinner" is not your core identity. You are nothing less than a follower of the King of kings. Begin to live like it, no matter what life brings to you and no matter how dark your interior. Bring the truth of your justification to bear upon your daily sanctification.

Calling the whole person:

Don't miss this calling of the whole man, Simon Peter, at a place and time when he was split and severed from active discipleship. He was already adjusting to a benchwarmer's complacency. Simon was doing what wounded souls do: he was retreating to what he knew for sure, going back to doing what was safe, predictable, and risk-free. He had stopped longing for the summit. He had stopped ascending.

He went back to fishing. His dysfunctional theme song was the default soundtrack of the Simon life.

Jesus called Simon to join with Peter, to become the conjoint man, who not only trusts Jesus with his sin theoretically and theologically but trusts Jesus with his failings on a daily basis. His self-definition was half true but fully debilitating. God, through Christ, came to make a new man, progressively and faithfully more and more conformed to the image of His Son.

Living "this precious faith" for me, for you, will require the joining of what is often split. We will be drawn into the grace that evokes deep trust, and produces strength. Simon will be transformed into Peter. This will demand full participation and trust for me and you, as it did for Peter. Like ascending those handholds on the climbing wall at the gym, our strength and tenacity will be tested. But when clinging to a slippery knob or gaining a toehold on some tiny bump, it is obvious that they are bolted to a much more massive superstructure. Behind the wall are substantial steel beams, supporting the entire surface.

When we declare that faith is anchored in God, we mean that it is bolted to the massive and unshakable purposes of God in Christ Jesus. That "a righteousness from God" (Rom. 3:21), objectively established, stands behind our quavering grip on faith. This is the solidity of the faith Peter points to. Peter, the gung ho zealot, the cheerleading promise maker, had learned to receive the grace he did not deserve and could not earn. His subjective neediness, great and desperate as it was, had ceased being the foundation of his faith. Instead, it was the foundation built on his Savior's love, the Lord's completed demonstration of justice and mercy, which established and held Peter.

Thirty challenging and adventurous years after his call, Peter's faith has been ruggedly tested and has proved to be alive and vibrant. Peter has made the simplest, most humble choice each day of his life. It's the choice I must make: "Jesus, I trust you with my twisted motives, my outsized fears, my convoluted pathologies. I trust you not only for eternity but for the hard choices of this day. I trust you because of the work already accomplished and for the work still in progress."

As with Peter, a person of frailty and failure like me can become a trophy of his grace. Faith is where the journey begins.

For personal application:

1. What do you mean when you refer to "my faith?"

2. Has there been a time when disappointments and hardships have shaken your faith?

3. Does ongoing trouble signal that you don't have enough faith?

4. What is immovable bedrock for your faith?

5. What have you experienced that made you cling to faith as if your life depended on it?

---

[1] For deeper exploration of this important issue see *Where Is God When It Hurts?* by Philip Yancey; *The Problem of Pain* by C. S. Lewis

3

Lead Climbing

Add to your faith Goodness...

—2 Peter 1:5

Handhold #2: Goodness

"It is the plain old Christianity that I teach," said John Wesley (1703–1791).

John Wesley's central understanding of Christianity was that individual redemption leads to social regeneration. He believed that the main purpose of the Bible is to show sinners their way back to God by the sacrifice of Christ. This is what he preached, but he also understood that social changes are an inevitable by-product and a useful piece of evidence of conversion. Because of the preaching of the gospel, the high moral principles set forth in Scriptures slowly began to take root in people's minds. Wesley believed that God's Word calls for the salvation of the individual souls. It also gives us firm ordinances for national existence and a common social life under God—these were his goals, and he never lost sight of them.

John Wesley's life was a triumph of God's grace. Under physical and verbal attack thousands of times, never once did he lose his temper. He loved his enemies, and do what they

would, they could not make him discourteous or angry. It is
no exaggeration to say that Wesley instilled into the British
people a new and biblical concept of courage and heroism. His
tranquil dignity, the absence of malice and anger, and above
all, the evidence of God's Spirit working in his life, eventually
disarmed his enemies and won them for Christ. Soldiers,
sailors, miners, fishermen, smugglers, industrial workers,
thieves, vagabonds, men, women, and children listened
intently, in apt reverent attention, gradually removed their hats
and knelt, often emotionally overcome, as he pointed these
thousands upon thousands to God's grace. For more than fifty
years, Wesley fed the Bible, the Word of life, to drink-sodden,
brutalized, and neglected multitudes.

Wesley understood the Bible demands that individual
conversion should lead to changes in society. He strongly
campaigned against slavery, smuggling, bribery, and corruption.
He fearlessly criticized aspects of the penal system and
prisons. He campaigned against the near-medieval methods of
medicine. He had a practical interest in electricity, vocational
training for the unemployed, the raising of money to clothe
and feed prisoners, to buy food, medicine, fuel, and tools for
the helpless and the aged. He preached heaven but he believed
that nature was God's gift to us, and therefore work was noble
and science was essential.[1]"

Author, teacher, adventurer, and mountain climber,
Tim Hansel was seated on a plane reading his New
Testament when the woman next to him asked, "Sir, are
you a Christian?" His answer is memorable and a lesson
in itself: "Yes, ma'am," he replied, "right down to my toes.
Right down the marrow of my bones."[2] His open-faced
declaration pulls back the curtain to display a holistic
picture of Christian discipleship that is seldom seen by
the casual observer or the merely curious. It portrays that
following Jesus is not just static adherence to orthodoxy, or
detached, cerebral assent. It is not merely Sunday activities

nor even strenuous moral conformity to a new value system. Being a disciple is a transformational commitment. It is a life given over, given up, and given to, an unceasing quest. This is Christianity embraced comprehensively, with no walled-off compartments, no reservations, no limits. It is head and heart, body and soul, theology and lifestyle all entwined. Yes, ma'am!

The woman receiving this answer must have been surprised, perhaps even shocked. Her casual question might have garnered just a mumbled affirmation or a philosophical feint, such as, "That depends on what you mean by 'Christian.'" Refreshingly, Hansel was instantly all in, like he had been just waiting to pounce. But besides the raw energy of this response, there is something else unusual about it.

Popular culture is unaccustomed, or perhaps purposely deaf, when it occasionally hears what a Christian, a true Christ follower, is *for*. The culture, and the media, it is safe to say, seems to think that Bible-believing, Christ-following disciples are defined by what they are against, not what they are for. High-profile marches, referenda, petitions, and radio talk shows clearly highlight the moral issues of our day, like abortion, homosexual rights, illegal immigration, curriculum wars, or a dozen other important, and controversial, concerns. Christ followers, rightly or wrongly, fairly or unfairly, are often pasted with labels regarding their stance on these issues. And quite naturally, Christians are most often painted with a broad brush, usually caricatured as angry, militant, oppositional, and against. The whole lot is unfortunately perceived by many as a bunch of religious contrarians, people who just love to throw their weight around while appealing to a higher power for unquestioned moral superiority. Jesus followers are dismissed as "againsters," naysayers, and obscurantist grumblers with nothing better to do. So the popular culture largely believes.

But what if true Christ followers became known for that they are *for*, not just for what they are against? What if, in fact, the watching culture began to see that disciples have many better things to do, many good things to be, and that this pervasive goodness is more—much more—than going to Sunday school or signing a petition: it is the very aroma of their Master wafting subversively into the culture. This is the real deal, the "down to my toes" kind of radical *goodness* that our coach Peter wants to encourage. His is a positive, aerobic, and forward-leaning kind of spiritual life that does not idle away its horsepower in privatized mulling. This faith springs out; it walks into; it climbs higher; it permeates the unsuspecting world. It answers life's questions with startling energy and intriguing commitment. So we may be as startled as this airline passenger when Peter begins his list of life skills that are to be added to faith.

"Make every effort to add to your faith *goodness*" (2 Pet. 1:5; emphasis added).

Not strictness. Not against-ness. Not defensiveness. Not resistance or contrariness. Add goodness right down to your toes. Peter is doing more than suggesting. He is inciting every believer to become more and more proficient in living out the goodness that God's Spirit has put in us. "He has given us his very great and precious promises, so that through them you may participate in the divine nature and escape the corruption in the world caused by evil desires" (2 Pet. 1:4).

Reading Peter's thoughts in sequence, it is not a stretch to conclude that as we participate in what we are *for*, we will receive the power to escape and resist what we, and the Lord, are *against*. But the movement Peter portrays is profoundly proactive and positive. It is primarily, and seminally, *for*, and secondarily *against*. Exercising the Spirit's endowments will rescue us from the world's enticements and the old nature's pitfalls. On a practical level, it will startle the person in the next seat, or next cubicle, or the next crisis, with an indomitable and pervasive goodness that the world seldom sees. Sadly, many believers do not perceive the influence of this life skill that Peter wants to teach us.

I admit that when I first reflected on Peter's list of life skills to add to faith, I believed this first one gave the whole challenge a weak start. It sounded wimpy and syrupy, kind of like "Be nice." Be good, don't cause problems, raise your hand before speaking, don't rock the boat, say "Excuse me" when you sneeze, mow your lawn, recycle, and be a good tipper. Be a good boy. Be a good girl. Be harmless, invisible, and silent. My mental image of goodness made me cynically wonder: do we really need special revelation, with apostolic authority, to teach simple third-grade citizenship and civility?

My respect for Peter's muscularity was restored when I began to look into the word he uses here. The word is *arete*, a rich Greek word often translated "virtue." It means moral excellence, and in a broader sense, it describes anything that properly fulfills its function. The goodness Peter is encouraging is anything but an insipid niceness, or a Pollyanna goodness.

As we climb toward greater effectiveness and spiritual fruitfulness, our faith is to be supplemented with a noticeable movement outward, toward our world. It is to evidence itself in a lifestyle, and a personal demeanor, of goodness. This is no small thing. Think about how the words *good* and *goodness* are used in the Bible, and it becomes huge!

Measuring goodness:

There are at least three ways to measure the size and majesty of this character trait. First of all, goodness is the size of God Himself. The table grace we said at every supper as I was growing up was, "O give thanks unto the Lord, for He is *good*, and his mercy endures forever" (Ps. 106:1; emphasis added). God retains and exercises all His attributes continuously and simultaneously. But permeating God's justice, his omnipotence, or His love, or even his wrath, is goodness. Every aspect of God is saturated with goodness. He is good. All the time. My faith in Him is to make me, in some small measure, like that pervasive goodness within my sphere of influence.

The second measure of goodness is this: it is the sum of all creation. When God culminated His works of creation, revealing His majesty and glory for the entire universe to exude, He chose a summary word. "It is good." In fact, God said, "It was very good" (Gen. 1:31). God's creation wasn't like so many of my projects, where I cover my imperfections by intoning: "That'll do for now. We'll improve on it later, or fix it when it breaks again." No, God looked at His entire universe and chose a word that bespoke its moral, biological, purposeful, beautiful completeness: "It was good." Every discrete, created entity was good in itself, and the entire whole was very good collectively, because it fulfilled its design and function.

A third, more personal way to get perspective on this great word *goodness* happens when we realize that this is the word that undergirds God's purposes for me—his purpose in redemption and sanctification. The motivation for personal devotion, sacrifice, and daily worship is that it will "prove what God's will is—his *good*, pleasing and perfect will" (Rom. 12:2; emphasis added). This word also describes the rewards of following Christ and the personal satisfactions found in obedience: "Every *good*, and perfect gift is from above, coming down from the Father of lights…" (James 1:17; emphasis added).

Gaining the measure of this word caused me to be much more interested in its challenging implications and its muscular applications. It is the next right thing to add to what can easily become a silent, privatized faith that hunkers down in the ghettoized isolation of a merely cerebral belief system. Peter chose this word carefully, placing it strategically in his proposed skill set for the believer. It is obvious that he intends this goodness to be a motive of the cleansed heart, an influencer of our culture, and a legacy of the living body of Christ in the world. Faith outs itself in outward, influential, irrepressible goodness in and toward the world.

We highlighted John Wesley's life and ministry in the opening monograph. From 1739 to his death in 1791, Wesley proved tireless. He rose every morning at four o'clock and preached his first sermon, often in a town square or at the mouth of a mine, by 5:00 a.m. He organized hundreds of local Methodist societies from the converts of this preaching. He traveled a quarter of a million miles on horseback and in a small chaise. Weather could not stop him. Dangerous roads never daunted him. Sleeping on stone floors and bearing the indignities of hurled obstacles from his detractors, he always pressed forward. The inner fire of his spiritual life was matched by an unprecedented output, unreachable by most mere mortals. He preached at least forty-five thousand sermons and wrote or contributed to more than three hundred and thirty books. John Wesley is the very definition of proactive goodness surging from the life of a devoted disciple. Learn from his example, but don't try to match his pace stride-for-stride.

The scale of this word *goodness* is as big as life, and the example we should follow is that of the Master. The goal is to fully function on earth as a representative of our good sovereign in heaven. The challenge is to display the transformed life of a totally new person to a watching and needy world.

By pondering the wealth of this word, I become aware of the risks involved in such visible, magnanimous, and far-reaching goodness. This discipline of goodness is counterculture. It is anti-flesh. Aspiring to this attribute will jolt us out of private reverie and into visible and vulnerable practice of our faith in the real world, with real people. Big talking—even big theologizing—will not substitute for goodness on the ground, in real time, in the real world.

This actual practice of goodness is like the feeling that rock climbers call "exposure." It's that gut check of nerve and will when moves deemed strenuous and impressive in the gym require real skin on the line and raw courage two hundred feet from the ground. Talk and strategy are useless unless they are implemented in real time, under visible and palpable risk.

I well remember my introduction to real rock climbing. It began safely enough in the secure envelope of the classroom. Robin held class in a barn, instructing all of us in basic terms, knots, commands, and procedures. He showed us how to belay each other from above and demonstrated to each of us that a good belay could hold our weight in case we slipped. He inspired confidence. Armed with that knowledge, we hiked out to the "pit," a sandstone arroyo with a variety of cliffs and boulders where we could apply our newfound expertise. I made my first climb on a forty-foot cliff, belayed from above by Robin, who was himself tied into the solid rock by anchor bolts. Every safety measure was in place. The climb was a purely athletic test. I never thought twice about falling or danger because I was "top-roped." I concentrated on handholds and footholds. It was a piece of cake. I was ready for a real challenge: something higher, harder, and more demanding.

That challenge came a week later. Now we were high in the Sierra Nevada mountains of northern California, and I, the neophyte climbing "leader," found myself halfway up a nearly vertical chute. The handholds were plentiful, the granite was sharp and strong, and the day was sparkling. But when I got about fifty feet up the chute, I realized that the ledge toward which I was climbing was not flat but sloped. That meant I would not be able to rest or belay the rest of my team up to join me. The security I had envisioned suddenly evaporated. I had no protection: pitons and cams that can be lodged into cracks to provide safety. Retracing my progress was impossible. Worse yet, I looked down. The exposure gave me cottonmouth. My knees began to shake in spasms, cynically called "sewing machine leg" in climber-speak. Suddenly, the risk I had been accruing with every upward move came home to me. This was no longer a clinic in athletic prowess. It was a life-endangering predicament. By some miracle, I managed to control my quaking legs and cramping hands, and move laterally, ascending another thirty feet to a wide ledge. Then and there I learned, in my puddle of exhaustion and relief, the difference between "lead climbing" and "top rope" climbing. It's all about exposure.

When rock climbers are tackling a major rock face, like the legendary El Capitan in Yosemite National Park, their strategy is efficient and very simple. They break down the climb into stages they call "pitches." A pitch can be anything from a forty- to one-hundred-foot section of the wall. This is the epitome of reaching an ultimate goal by means of intermediate and short-term goals. Pitch by pitch, the climbers laid siege to the wall. But the catch is, somebody has to lead. Somebody has to "lead climb" above their "protection" to advance the climb. This lead climbing of a pitch is the true test of the climber. It is skill, strength, and partnership in the face of increasingly threatening exposure. Lead climbing high on the wall means that climbing is no longer an exercise merely in gymnastic proficiency. It is raw physical courage in the face of yawning, potentially deadly exposure.

With proper use of protection, a skilled climber minimizes his risks. As he climbs, he places wedges, chocks, and cams into cracks, and clips his rope into them. But there is no way to eliminate all risk. As he is belayed from below, this means that if he falls, he will fall past his last point of protection until the rope arrests him. His fall can be anywhere from ten to thirty feet, depending on the placement of protection. Though this kind of fall is not fatal, it is, in the droll language of climbing, "unpleasant." Especially if you are 1,200 feet above the valley floor and your life is dependent on a half-inch rope or a one-eighth-inch nubbin of a foothold.

What I learned on the first day of climbing is that anybody can top-rope climb. Even those afraid of heights can steel themselves with the knowledge that they are held from above, and that slips or falls will be caught instantly and without injury. It's like riding in those little kiddie cars at the amusement park. They move around the course, but they are guided by a track that ensures a predetermined destination. Top-rope climbing is fun, but it's like training wheels on a bicycle.

No exceptions:

When Peter lists "goodness" as the next handhold for the disciple following an initial faith, he is thrusting every disciple into lead climbing. This first life skill measures our courage and commitment instantly. It is breathtaking and knee knocking. It is an immediate challenge to accept the exposure and vulnerability of lead climbing. He points out the implications in his first letter: "Live such good lives among the pagans that, though they accuse you of doing wrong, they may see your good deeds and glorify God on the day he visits us" (1 Pet. 2:12).

Prepare to jump into the deep end. Point your kayak into the maelstrom of rapids. Step out of the greenhouse. Don't hide in the incubator. Take the next pitch of the climb. It's your turn to lead. Risk the exposure of ridicule, resistance, and potential slipups. Live your faith with visible, unquenchable goodness in a world determined to pull you down.

But hold on one second. Though Peter is not counseling every Christ follower to delay his sortie into the real world by first spending four years in graduate school, neither is he sending us off like lemmings to needlessly plunge to our deaths. Peter was, after all, schooled by Jesus, who warned, "In this world you will have trouble. If the world hates you, keep in mind that it hated me first. If they persecuted me, they will persecute you also" (John 16:33, 15:18, 15:20). Peter himself lived with the Lord's own prophecy regarding his excruciating future. So we can be confident that Peter is well aware of the conditions these believers will face when they "out" their faith in goodness.

Visible and generous good works, pulling upward against the pernicious gravity of a fallen world, will require consistent moral courage, combined with tactical shrewdness. Without this mental toughness and practical preparation, our spasms of goodness will be mere quixotic forays without redemptive impact. So before we jump into a "do list" of heroic activities and spectacular sacrifices, let's look at some necessary training and preparation in order to sustain the kind of goodness Peter calls us to demonstrate.

Goodness is only sustainable from a core strength that exudes from sound spiritual healthiness. A heart of humility is at the center of this hygienic regimen. Goodness in our dangerous world doesn't fail for lack of IQ, dollars, or good intentions. It fails because the hearts of Christ followers don't desire and cultivate goodness at the deepest level. We are easily distracted by the challenge, caught up in the planning, or grieved by the need, but we too often neglect the condition of our own hearts. This is the wellspring (Prov. 4:23). It is the pump through which all loyalty, wisdom, and courage must flow. For goodness to thrive, the heart must be clean, clear, and strong. "Surely you desire truth in the inner parts; you teach me wisdom in the inmost place." (Ps. 51:6). The courage to lead climb begins in a place no one will ever see, except God. It is nurtured in a humble heart.

This heart preparation is solitary. It is must be honest and guileless. This vigilant discipline is recurrent and lifelong. The guarded heart that wants to practice goodness confesses deeply that "nothing good lives in me, that is, in my sinful nature" (Romans 7:18). So it trains on daily grace, received in daily humility, fed by daily reminders to "hate what is evil; cling to what is good" (Rom. 12:9). There is a conscious striving, first and foremost, to love the good and hate the evil at the deepest level, especially when it gurgles up right inside my inmost being.

Long before tackling the challenges out in the world, the true disciple faces the slipperiness of his own heart. To rush into the void armed with fresh altruism and entrepreneurial adrenaline will only lead to inevitable breakdowns higher on the climb. This impulsiveness will bring harm to those who follow us and depend upon us. Doing good without first treasuring goodness in the heart will only hasten the split in our core that is called hypocrisy: trying to be, and trying even harder to appear to be, someone we are not. Hypocrisy has a very short shelf life. As risk and fatigue increase, the disintegrated, unexamined heart will renege when the next lead requires fresh courage.

We must be careful here. All these muscular, outdoor allusions may lead to the false conclusion that lead climbing is only for the elite, the few. But Peter had no such restrictions in mind. He is calling the whole church, and we are just beginning the list of life skills. The implication is clear. Ascent into greater and greater spiritual effectiveness (2 Pet. 1:8) is not magical. It is not a product of secrets, pedigrees, or bravado. Spiritual effectiveness and productivity are the product of a process, and great reward is promised, but the unprepared will quickly be outmatched in the real world of gravity and risk.

I experienced the sting of ill-preparedness one summer on a trip to Scotland. Fortunately, the wound was only to my ego. We were a team of eight on a short-term mission trip in partnership with a church in Glenrothes, a town near Edinburgh. As our time with them came to a close, we were invited to the nearby town of Newborough that was hosting the Highland Games. The green was staked out with a quarter-mile oval for foot races and bike races. We watched huge men in kilts toss the caber, a twelve-foot log, and hurl the thirty-five-pound weight over a bar. There were Scottish folk dancers and bagpipes. But our truest taste of Scotland was the finale of the Highland Games: the tug-of-war. They were calling for teams to sign up, so we looked at each other and said, "Hey, why not!" We had been to summer camp. We were reasonably athletic, and we had a secret weapon. Karry was a two-hundred-eighty-pound former offensive lineman for the Colorado Buffalos. We figured we would just tie the rope around him as an anchor, and it would be game over.

Confidently, we dubbed ourselves the "Glenrothes All-Stars." Our confidence lasted right up until we saw the other team. They were all nearly as big as Karry. Towns sponsored these all-star teams. They wore rugby jerseys with the names of their sponsoring pubs and car dealerships. Each one had a wide leather belt like a weightlifter. Most ominous of all were their boots. Hobnail boots. As if that weren't enough, these boots had a three-inch metal spur sticking straight out of the heel so that they could dig into the slippery grass turf. It was then that we noticed our loafers and Keds and the wet grass.

We approached the rope like lambs to the slaughter. The hooting crowd was beside itself, but we smiled with good-natured American sportsmanship. The judge lined us up, five to a side, and called "Pull!" We held them to a stalemate! The rope was taut. Our grip was firm. We leaned our weight and pulled with all our might. Then, the whistle blew, and we instantly realized that the first command to "pull" was only a way to take the slack out of the rope. At the whistle, their captain bawled "*Pull!*" and we slid across that wet turf like Bambi on a frozen lake.

As if that weren't bad enough, while the crowd howled and whistled, we learned from the referee that this contest, to be fair, was a best two out of three. So, we had another chance to be utterly humiliated. We were dragged to ignominious defeat again, in record time. Grass-stained, embarrassed, and publicly defeated, we just wanted to get out of town as quickly as possible. When they asked where we came from, we said, "Canada."

People who are unprepared and inexperienced are easily defeated by the realities on the ground and ready prey for those who are practiced in their craft. Defeated people don't want to repeat the attempt. Visible failure makes us just want to stay anonymous and get private as quickly as possible. After a thumping, it is completely counterintuitive to want to risk again.

Real-world risk:

That's why lead climbing with muscular goodness requires courage. The risks are obvious, and the powers against goodness are well outfitted. Goodness is not a health club workout: it is a real world risk.

That's what Rebecca sees on a regular basis. She and her husband, Andrew, live under constant exposure, threat, and risk just because they infuse a ray of goodness into the dark street life in Albania. They oversee the Children's Day Center and the Safe Home in the city of Korce. Rebecca started this work as a short-term missionary. She noticed young girls, age six to ten, and pre-teens on the street after school, and simply began offering them a warm, safe place to spend a few hours each day.

That simple offering of goodness began to uncover the dark truth that lay beneath. These girls were routinely sold as sex slaves. Their own fathers were often the perpetrators. Compassion soon led to intervention. Rebecca frequently becomes the catalyst for authorities to remove children from their homes for their own safety. Some men have been arrested and have gone to trial for murder, sex trafficking, and rape. A few have ended up in prison. What began as the compassionate urgency to do something—anything— to help, has now become a haven of goodness for over a dozen years. But not without risk.

These interventions are not welcomed by these predators, nor the sex trafficking network. Guileless goodness is like a candle in an evil wind. Rebecca and Andrew have no protection except the sovereign hand of God. But they keep giving themselves away, lead climbing above what is safe. They keep walking into heartbreaking stories, exploitative systems, and scenarios of brutal abuse not knowing exactly what to do. But they do the next right thing. And goodness shines through that darkness.

You and I may not operate on such a stark dividing line of light and darkness. However, every exercise of goodness goes against gravity. It opposes the pervasive pull of this world's current. It is never neutral, nor entirely safe.

Yes, practicing goodness might cause us to be hurt, overwhelmed, or embarrassed on the fields of play. Having taken the risk and expended the energy to lead climb, it hurts to slip, fall past your protection, and be slammed against the rock face. It doesn't take many repetitions of this experience before we resolve to stay safe, hunker down, and let someone else challenge the mountain.

Our life coach, Peter, is neither naive nor silent about the nature of the world we inhabit. He doesn't leave us guessing about the dangers of our climb, the intent of the evil one, or the slipperiness of our own flesh. That's why Peter is rallying our faith to make a firm and irrevocable commitment to this first handhold. His challenge to every disciple is: "Make every effort to add to your faith goodness" (1 Pet. 1:5). Choose this strenuous first discipline with full alertness. Grasp the handhold with resolve and strength. Prepare for the sharp and abrasive realities of ascent. Commit, down to your toes, to be a Christ follower.

For personal application:

1. What practice of goodness in the world inspires you as an evidence of God's working through his people?

2. Despite all the moral outrages that deserve resistance and protest, what are you for, not just against?

3. Is there an initiative of goodness that you need to lead? What are the risks?

4. How do you keep your heart clean so that goodness is deeper than just nice activity?

5. Where and when in your life is this handhold needed?

---

[1] Excerpted from Vishal Mangalwadi, *The Book That Made Your World: How the Bible Created the Soul of Western Civilization* (Nashville, Tenn.: Thomas Nelson, 2011) pp 265–268

[2] Tim Hansel, *Holy Sweat* (Waco, Texas: Word Books, 1987) p 28

4

<hr>

Anchor Points

*Add to your faith goodness; and
to goodness, knowledge…*

Handhold #3: Knowledge

 When my wife and I moved into our first home, we learned more than a few lessons the hard way. A little knowledge goes a long ways. Conversely, lacking essential knowledge brings frustration and stress.

Barely qualifying for our mortgage and still adjusting to the surprise expenses of home ownership, we had scant resources for home improvements. So we decided to start with wallpaper on the entry wall of our living room.

A small paint and wallpaper store had just opened in our neighborhood. Mr. Carney, the owner, was the definition of patience and helpfulness as we leafed through huge tomes of wallpaper options. We finally decided on our pattern, bought the paper and the paste, and headed out the door with complete instructions. That evening, eager to beautify our space, we quickly and easily—to our delighted surprise— papered our wall. With outlet covers reattached, and furniture back in place, we went to bed with deep satisfaction. We had wallpapered together, our marriage had survived, and our home had become an expression of "us."

Joanne's shriek the next morning brought me bounding from bed. "Look at this! It's a disaster," she said with a horrified look on her face. As I rounded the corner, I saw six neatly rolled cylinders of wallpaper on the floor and a naked beige wall. The glue hadn't held. The wallpaper was defective. Our money was wasted! We decided to demand a refund. We gathered up our wallpaper and our indignation and drove to the store. We were polite but clearly registered with Mr. Carney that we were definitely dissatisfied customers.

As we broached the subject of a refund, Mr. Carney gently interrupted with a simple question.

"Did you size the wall?"

"Well, of course," I answered. "I measured it side to side and top to bottom."

"I'm sorry," he quietly replied, "perhaps you don't understand the use of the word *sizing* as it applies to wallpaper." Admittedly, I had breezed by the section on sizing in the instructions, thinking I had already been there, done that. I was intent on pressing into the adventure of room transformation!

"Sizing," Mr. Carney quietly continued, leaving no assumption unexamined, "is necessary on any painted wall. You must size the wall, meaning pretreating it with sealer so that the painted wall doesn't suck the moisture out of the wallpaper paste too quickly. If it dries too quickly, it won't adhere, and your wallpaper might peel." He looked silently at me with innocent, bespectacled eyes, piercingly and wordlessly asking, "Do you know what you are doing? Did you jump into wallpapering without reading the instructions?" I mumbled something like, "Oh, so what type of sizing would you recommend?" We drove home humbled but schooled with essential knowledge.

Peter is coaching us: add to your deep commitment to follow God, and your prodigious efforts to live out its implications a large dose of knowledge. Otherwise you labor in vain to function effectively in your world. You will react in indignation to failed dreams. You will be discouraged by adverse winds against your progress. You will blame others. You will quit because everything seems to go contrary to your view of the world. You will endanger yourself and others, not to mention squandering time, energy, and resources.

Peter now draws attention to our grip on "knowledge." It's the next logical progression in this ascent which begins with faith and aspires to practice the goodness of God Himself in this resistant environment. Peter knows if we hurl ourselves into the next challenge with deep devotion and inspiring courage but lack a handhold on knowledge, the unrelenting gravity of real life will render us wounded and beaten. In the climbing world, there is zero tolerance for lack of knowledge. It's called falling. It hurts—sometimes fatally. So get ready to be a learner for life in order to keep your grip and maintain your progress.

When we enroll in the apostle Peter's school of climbing, it isn't a competition. The slogan of this school is Everybody Up! The goals, the skills, the curriculum, and the encouragements are open to anyone so that everyone can ascend toward full maturity. It's not every man for himself but every one for each one. Like his compatriot Paul, who wants every disciple to "grow up into Christ" (Eph. 4:15), Peter also wants every believer to "participate" actively in his own maturing process (2 Pet. 1:4).

These handholds are not measuring the attainment of a higher position or the achievement of special privilege. They neither quantify one's greater inherent worth to God nor signal the attainment of freedom from the troubles of this world. Every disciple needs every skill, and each must summon the right handhold at a moment's notice. True disciples want to learn how to apply these skills— for themselves and for everyone else on the climbing team. This array of life skills is as necessary at the beginning of the climb—one foot off the ground—as it is after many pitches of climbing. Each challenge in life calls for the practiced application of the right, secure handhold.

Peter places "knowledge" like an oscillating fan between faith and goodness. Knowledge constantly stirs the air and balances the environment for holistic decision-making. Peter's own life-transforming encounter with Jesus implanted a dauntless calling: an unshakable faith and a fearless trust in his Master. He was forever changed and finally ready to live out his pledge to lay down his life for Christ. The maturing Peter, however, recognizes that only knowledge can steer this courage and meter this energy over the long haul.

In the previous chapter, we saw that goodness calls every disciple toward his inherent fear: exposure and risk. Everything in us wants to minimize that risk. Experience with the fear and blunt force of gravity teaches us that slips and mistakes hurt. We naturally want mistake-proof backups, belays, and scab-free ascents. Knowledge does not erase risk, but it is that essential skill which blends understanding with courage. Knowledge constantly braces us with both an accurate realization of the dangers and fresh confidence to keep us climbing. The going is tough, but knowledge coaches the tough to keep going.

> *Climbing can be dangerous…Climbers who have had long, safe careers are alive today because they understand the risks and behave accordingly, not because they are lucky. Most climbers don't place their sport in the same*

category as other so-called risk sports, like bungee-jumping or hang-gliding. Instead, they see their game as one of control, of mental and physical achievement. They don't toss their fate to the winds or play variations of Russian roulette[1].

As they say, there are old climbers and bold climbers, but there are no old, bold climbers. Climbers use anchors to manage the risk of their adventures. In today's ecological, leave-no-trace ethos, climbers use cleverly designed wedges, chocks, and cams as belaying points. Whatever the technology, the principle remains: fixed anchors along the way serve a dual purpose—they not only protect us from falling but they also instill in us the courage to keep ascending.

Put another way, knowledge is like the big bubble of a bell curve. On the leading extreme are those who are overconfident in their faith and see no dangers or slow downs ahead. On the trailing edge are those who have become risk averse, hyper-vigilant with warnings, and oversupplied with protections. The bountiful middle, where knowledge draws these extremes together, is the next right thing in the disciple's profile. It keeps him from being "ineffective and unproductive" (1 Pet. 1:8) by pulling the extremes of our human nature into a coordinated deployment of skillful strength.

Faith without knowledge is motorcycle daredevil Evel Knievel hurtling over the fountains of Caesar's palace and shattering himself irreparably—a costly and harebrained stunt using his body as a human projectile. Conversely, goodness without knowledge is a notebook full of good intentions petrified into inert, nanny Christianity of risk-averse niceness.

Note that knowledge is just one of eight handholds in Peter's repertoire. Knowing is not the sum total of the Christian life. However, unless we know, understand, and apply certain truths, our ascent toward maturity will be undermined by confusion and frustration. If we maintain false assumptions about the nature of the world, the nature of God, or the nature of ourselves, we will become discouraged, silent, or cynical when our assumptions are routinely contradicted by experience.

For example, it is a commonly held fiction that the following formula is true: God is good. I do good. Therefore, everything will be good. So we rush out to help the homeless, or feed the hungry, give generously, or intervene in a friend's failing marriage. Along the way, we discover legal liabilities and physical dangers we never anticipated, shocking ingratitude, questionable budget decisions, and alienation from a former friend. We do good by our children with Little League, summer camp, mission trips, Christian college, and much prayer, yet somewhere in their twenties they become de-churched, spiritually listless, and far from God. We tithe and pray and serve and sacrifice, but then our church leadership makes decisions that confound our vision for the body and takes it in directions we fear are unwise and uncomfortable.

Knowledge cures none of these problems. It is not the silver bullet that avoids complications, conundrums, and conflicts. But knowledge profoundly strengthens the mind to face up to reality. It stretches our capacity to understand hardships and to wait patiently when answers don't arrive on our timetable. Without biblical knowledge and a worldview that develops from it, we are sentenced to cling to expectations that cannot hold the size and weight of our experience. The weight of reality will drag us down, abrade our skin, and discourage our ascent.

Psychologists call this "cognitive dissonance." It's the mental stress of trying to hold two contradictory beliefs simultaneously. The following are experiences that cause this dissonance: I believe God is good so he will bless my business. But, my business is bankrupt. God answers prayer, and I've prayed for healing: my mom is dying of cancer. Good parenting results in thriving young adults: my child is directionless. Love never fails, and I still love her: divorce court convenes tomorrow.

Each time an anchor point of belief gives way and I get hurt I am much more likely to abandon the climb altogether, feeling that I have been duped into a dangerous and futile misadventure.

Josh McDowell captures this inner tension in a phrase: "The heart cannot rejoice in what the mind rejects as false." If the cognitive dissonance between what we believe in theory and what we "know" through experience becomes too great, or too frequent we will be tempted to lessen that tension by abandoning our belief. We will go with what we "know" in our hearts from observation and experience. Therefore, adding trustworthy, weather-proof knowledge is essential to sustaining our faith in an environment that often seems maddeningly disappointing and inscrutable.

Anchors for the mind:

When Peter calls us to "add knowledge," he is pointing us to anchors for our minds which will bear the weight of seemingly contrary evidence, random storms, and brutal setbacks. There are three anchor points that could change everything about how you confront your current challenge. What follows are three categories of essential knowledge for every disciple. They give us a grip on knowledge in every challenging situation. They can be instantaneously grasped by the newest convert, and are inexhaustibly strong for the deepest and the oldest follower of Christ.

The Peace Anchor

In Peter's first letter, he referred repeatedly to the need for knowledge. "Prepare your minds. . . for you know. . . be clear-minded" (1 Pet. 1:13, 1:18, 4:7). Eleven times in this second letter Peter repeats the theme of knowledge: "Even though you know...wholesome thinking...hard to understand...you already know this...guard against error... grow in the grace and knowledge of our Lord" (2 Pet. 1:12, 3:1, 3:16–18).

Of all the subjects and data that we should know, where do we begin? What did Peter mean when he said we have been given everything we need for life and godliness? Certainly he wasn't referring to the necessity of four courses in theology or a fluency in Greek. He was writing to people who had few books: perhaps only a copy of the Old Testament, or the Torah. He was writing to encourage dispersed and culturally alienated believers who had heard the Gospel and experienced the powerful change brought by the Holy Spirit. Now they are reading this circular letter as their sole fragment of what would become the New Testament. So this knowledge Peter refers to cannot imply a bookish degree program or even daily Bible reading. Many of his recipients were no doubt illiterate. How should they add knowledge in increasing measure?

The knowledge Peter refers to is their knowledge of the Gospel. "To those who through the righteousness of our God and Savior Jesus Christ have received a faith as precious as ours" (2 Pet. 1:1). What they knew is that God Himself had done something indescribably powerful and precious through the Savior, Jesus Christ. What the Old Testament prophets had foretold but their sin and the harsh world seemed to render impossible, God had accomplished in the person and work of Jesus. He made peace. He brought peace. He speaks peace. Peter writes life-giving encouragement: "Grace and *peace* be yours in abundance *through the knowledge* of God and of Jesus our Lord" (2 Pet. 1:2; emphasis added).

Just remembering this one name, this one person, and His stupendous accomplishment was enough to assure Peter's friends that everything necessary for life and salvation had already been accomplished. They have an anchor point in Christ's finished work on the cross that establishes something all human strength and effort can never offer: peace. Peace at the core. Peace despite every outward circumstance and every sinful failure.

The apostle Paul also develops the immovability of this anchor by grounding it in solid fact. This peace is not first a subjective sense of tranquility or a mind-over-matter toughness. It is a peace won in a battle against our enemy which by faith we can now enjoy.

"Therefore, since we have been justified through faith, *we have peace with God* through our Lord Jesus Christ" (Rom. 5:1; emphasis added).

The objectivity, indisputability, and immovability of this anchor of peace cannot be over emphasized. This is essential knowledge for the maddening, wounding, hard, and dangerous world in which our faith walks.

My friend Sam needs this knowledge. He is a growing disciple in many ways, a trophy of grace in a life with many disappointments and lots of pressure. But his stresses and thumps are made immeasurably harder and require much longer periods of recovery because he lacks this essential anchor point. He has no foundational peace. When trouble comes, he doesn't know who he is because he forgets what God has done. His experience shouts so loudly that he can't hear this truth.

Sam's emotional default position when he is fearful is to try much harder to regain peace. He equates rebuffs from his wife, or health problems, or financial setbacks as encrypted signals from God that he has tripped and fallen outside the family. "Now you've done it: all is lost," is the recurring message from his fearful heart. A kick in his spiritual shins, a stumble of weakness, or a disappointment of plans causes him to fall, not just to the ground, or off the curb, but over the precipice toward spiritual ruin—or so it seems to him. Every life trial pitches him into a spiritual abyss. He fears spiritual death, or irrecoverable loss, in every slip-up. Obviously this makes his infrequent forays toward exposure, risk, and personal investment tentative and short-lived. He has no core. Everything could fail at any moment, with catastrophe close behind.

How diametrically opposite this is to the message of the New Testament Gospel. Paul himself writes in one of Christendom's favorite verses that "trouble, hardship, persecution, famine, nakedness, danger, or sword cannot separate us from the love of Christ" (Rom. 8:38). Trouble does not exclude this core peace. Trouble doesn't mean that my relationship with God is broken, and now He's trying to "tell me something." But unless I know this peace about my belonging and identity with a deep assurance, the unexplainable, the unfair, the excruciating, and the unthinkable events of life will send me plunging into despair. Without the solid anchor of knowledge, and a firm grip on it, this awesome assurance of God's redemptive peace will not fortify the soul when threatened by trouble.

God, in pure grace, did not ignore sin—mine, yours, the world's—past or future. He did not forget about the horrors of despotic regimes, the heartbreak of infertility, the broken promises of a spouse, or the flailings of our nation's economy. When Christ died to make peace between a holy God and a renegade humanity, he calculated the cost and paid it all on the cross through Jesus's redeeming death. He paid my part and your part. He absorbed the entire collective, poisonous history of humanity gone mad. He atoned for all the injustices and horrors of war. He cleansed the toxic waste landfills of lust, greed, and envy. He redeemed the cesspools of shame, woundedness, and dysfunction. He made all this evil irrelevant to our relationship with Him because He conquered it by atonement. The incalculable record of heinous wrong that should have rendered me an enemy for eternity was cancelled by His payment on my behalf. God made that peace. My indelible identity now is "son" or "daughter." I am no longer an enemy, an orphan, or a project. I am home, and I have a secure future. The cross paid for that peace. The Gospel is the witness to that peace. The miracle of grace is that dead people were made alive. The guilty were pronounced innocent, and enemies were made into friends. Peace is here!

This is core biblical doctrine, and without sound knowledge of it, our strength will fail. No grip will remain strong without a respite. Knowledge of God's declaration of peace allows me to hang the weights of uncertainty, discouragement, and sorrow on Him. Jesus shouts from the resurrection and ascension: "I've got you! I will hold you. Nothing can ever change what I have accomplished for you!"This anchor works in the real world. Philippians 4:5b–7 is one very practical application.

"The Lord is near. Do not be anxious about anything, but in everything, by prayer and petition, with thanksgiving, present your requests to God. And the *peace of God will guard your hearts and minds in Christ Jesus.*" (emphasis added)

Peace is made by God, but peace is also applied by God. Here, Paul assures that in the flurry of "everything," we can know the peace God made on the cross is also the peace He can apply to a worried heart. This peace does not just stand like a landmark, austere and empirical. It is a transferrable and transportable peace that moves with us into today's mess. It is only when we know this objectively that we can experience it subjectively.

I can almost measure this peace by Brett's body language. Over the course of several years, I have watched his furtive and dour countenance transform into a joyful and eager involvement. He came to our men's group as an accomplished professional at the top of his game. But he didn't say much and left quickly at the close. His life was stalled. He was single and had no real friends. Being around Christian men in a Bible study was threatening. But he kept coming, and slowly began interacting.

At a lunch appointment, I heard part of his story. His wife had taken her own life fifteen years ago. He raised his daughters on his own while building up his business. Several failed relationships followed. Emotionally he was running on fumes. He felt guilty and angry, cheated by life. Then a friend did the simplest thing: they invited him to church where he began hearing the words of life explained. God began drawing him to Himself, and one day he melted. "I want more of what I'm feeling now," he said. Grace and salvation were explained. Forgiveness and freedom were embraced. Brett began to feel the burdens, wounds, and sorrows lifted. As his knowledge increased his faith became strong. That's when he began to come out of the shadows. His face brightened. His posture changed. His personality emerged.

The peace that God has given through repentance and salvation is now a realized and visible peace in Brett's daily vitality. God has put to rest the old fears, failures, and sorrows. Though peace eluded him for decades, Brett now walks expectantly because he knows he is loved, sought after, and reconciled by grace. Knowledge brings peace.

The Life Anchor

It's a marvel that rock climbers keep wanting greater challenges, more difficult routes, and unconquered heights. What seems unthinkable to acrophobics actually inspires the dreams of the alpinist. How can they not be consumed and paralyzed by the fear of falling? It is because they have intimate knowledge of the hazards and plan to place protection in the wall. This practical know-how mitigates both the objective danger and the subjective fear of falling.

This serves as a visual metaphor of our spiritual climb. We must understand and register the ultimate reality of death, but we must not overinflate its threat. This is the core beauty of the Gospel. Death is real, but redemption and eternity through Christ's victory are even more real. Death has lost its stinger. Daily, applied knowledge of this truth on a personal basis changes how I tackle daunting challenges and personal risks.

I'm clinging to this anchor even as I write this. My dad is on his deathbed just an arm's length away. The oxygen pump cycles every few seconds as Dad's openmouthed breathing continues, for the moment. His wrinkle-free skin is stretched over the skeletal ridges of his cheekbones. His ninety-four-year old skin is paper thin. Those once strong hands are now mere functionless appendages, unable to grip, point, or even scratch. The hospice nurse can read the signs and tells me that his symptoms foretell of his death within the next seven days.

Death is real. It is ugly. It hovers over my thoughts and emotions every minute. I know this. It is taking away the life mentor I've always treasured. It is stealing the wordsmith, the resident enthusiast, the preacher, and the mechanical wizard who shared so many of life's milestones with me. This is the father who brought me into this world and whose fingerprints are all over my history, my skills, my joys, and my purpose. Scrapbooks, pieces of furniture, his notebooks, and musings will never substitute for the real man who animated this earth. It's not pretty, and I don't like watching death's inexorable encroachment on the life that has exuded from this unique man. It stinks. But it's no surprise.

Knowledge of death is woven into every page of the Bible, starting in Genesis chapter 3, so there is no excuse for not knowing about it. To ignore or dismiss this knowledge is to live in fantasy. But knowing about death is not the end of the story. I know this as well because I believe the Savior died and rose again, conquering death. Death itself, and its ally of fear, has been defeated by the resurrection. The promise and the hope of life are anchored not just in the hope of resurrection but also in the fact of Jesus's resurrection.

"Since the children have flesh and blood, he too shared in their humanity so that by his death he might destroy him who holds the power of death—that is, the devil—*and free those who all their lives were held in slavery by their fear of death*" (Heb. 2:14–15; emphasis added).

One can keep climbing boldly as long as solid anchors are fastened to knowledge, but ascents will be overwhelmed with exhaustion and futility if we are hauling our greatest fear up every pitch of the climb. It's too great a burden to stare death in the face with each challenge, thinking that every important and essential thing hangs on each choice. The life anchor is driven into the bedrock assurance of Christ's victory so that everyday fears can be faced and overcome.

While the peace anchor focuses on the atonement paid, the life anchor fixes itself on the resurrection achieved. This anchor provides an emotional trump card to the loss of a loved one, or the worst medical diagnosis. The life anchor can keep you moving even during those asphyxiating hours and days in the waiting room of rejection. Being anchored into the life Jesus promised beyond this earthly life is not an escape to unreality but a strength to meet the harsh reality we face here and now.

How heartening to know that the apostle Paul himself grasped for this anchor when nothing was going right, and he lost his grip on his mission and ministry. He transparently recounts his reliance on this life anchor: "We were under great pressure, so that we despaired even of life. Indeed, in our hearts we felt the sentence of death" (2 Cor. 1:8b).

Paul's courage, strength, physical resilience, and perspective were spent. He had faced nothing but resistance, abandonment, and brutal persecution with little measurable progress. The sentence of death hung unbearably heavy on his shoulders. He sagged and wanted to quit. His initial vision had been obliterated by a dust storm of suffering and fear. But then he remembers what he knows! He rediscovers what Peter says we should seek in "increasing measure" throughout life. Paul reaches once again for the life anchor: "But this happened that we might not rely on ourselves, but on God, *who raises the dead. He has delivered us from such a deadly peril*" (2 Cor.1:9–10a; emphasis added).

Paul was driven by hardships to confront his worst-case scenario: the loss of his very existence, his physical life. But right there, God's anchor held him, reminded him, and redeployed him. These experiences, and this life, are not all there is! God's ultimate victory is the resurrection of all who put their faith in Him. This knowledge does not anesthetize the pain, but it does provide much needed perspective and proportion. What was true for Paul under persecution is true for you with your special needs child, your sputtering business, your prodigal teen. As the song accurately summarizes, "Because He lives, I can face tomorrow."

I was enjoying a midwinter escape to a friend's Wisconsin cabin. Lying on the coffee table was a new book: *The Worst-Case Scenario Handbook*.[2] Its contents fascinated me. It gave advice from experts about how to survive a shark attack, deliver a baby in a taxi, or what to do when your parachute fails to open. Killer bees and poisonous snake bites were the subjects of chapters. Then I read the forward, which stated, "Warning: When life is imperiled or a dire situation is at hand, safe alternatives may not exist. To deal with a worst-case scenario, we insist that the best course of action is to consult a professionally trained expert. Do not attempt to undertake any of the actions described in this book yourself!"

The authors went on to disclaim any liability for any injury. And finally, they wrote, "We do not guarantee that the information contained herein is complete, safe, or accurate."

How ironic, even irresponsible, to purport to give critical advice at the brink of death and then disclaim any ownership of it! Followers of Jesus and readers of the Bible will never find such disclaimers. Instead, we are admonished to believe with even greater confidence what we already know, and especially in times of crisis. We are drawn back, again and again, to the anchors that do not move when the most terrifying threats appear. The Life Anchor holds because "Christ has indeed been raised from the dead" (1 Cor. 15:20).

The Hope Anchor

In the crux, at the point of risk and fear, what else do we need to know? We need to know that the future is not up for grabs, nor is my life drifting on the winds of randomness. We need to know there is hope and how to hope. We need to know that hope is generated by gripping the solid truth behind God's revelation and understanding that He is still in control. Hope is not merely some wistful optimism or a fleeting emotional high. It is a trustworthy spiritual anchor drilled into a biblical worldview. We need to know that creation, its beginning, middle, and end is accurately described and powerfully steered toward the good end God intends. I need to know that my journey through God's creation has not slipped off the radar screen.

When we add knowledge anchored in hope, we are empowered to keep pressing on. We gain the passion and incentive to tackle hard and seemingly obstinate challenges. The compelling story of Joseph in the Old Testament (Gen. 37–51) is the track record of a man who was fueled by hope. Joseph knew every kind of hardship: betrayal, abuse, slavery, false accusation, imprisonment. He was supremely talented, hardworking, and gifted. But he found himself repeatedly trapped, stuck, jailed, and alone. He had to make hard choices under harsh conditions. Even so he had hope. And though he lived a thousand years before Peter, Joseph embodied the words Peter was to write: "For it is commendable if a man bears up under the pain of unjust suffering because he is conscious of God" (1 Pet. 2:19).

Being conscious of God is another way of knowing God's providence as a sustaining handhold. Being conscious of God transforms hope from a fleeting emotion to a knowledgeable volition. This is a hope that knows that God's attention is not diverted to something or someone else more important than me. It is a knowing on a devotional level, in the midst of pain and uncertainty, that God has a plan and a purpose for me. When this is known, it burns as hope in the soul, hope in the exercise of options, and hope despite the headwinds of adversity.

Hope in God and what He has revealed acts like the air flowing over the upper surface of an airplane wing. It generates lift, and that activates the miracle of heavier-than-air objects actually taking flight. We can explain through physics how this principle of aerodynamics works, but the seat-of-the-pants experience of it is buoyancy, or lift. Hope provides this kind of invisible but powerful motivation to press on despite gravity. Hope buoys us to persevere again today when we are tired and don't know the final outcome.

This hope is a reservoir fed by the dual tributaries of God's special and general revelation. This huge supply of hope is what Harry Blamires *(The Christian Mind)*, Francis Schaeffer *(The God Who is There)* , Charles Colson *(How Now Should We Live)*, Ravi Zacharias *(Can Man Live Without God)*, and many others call the "biblical worldview." Everything that is true, accurate, discoverable, and mysterious finds its place in a fully orbed and humble knowledge of our world. Everything in it is moving toward His glorious completion. Every wrong and devilish catastrophe finds a framework in God's Word which helps us understand.

No, a biblical worldview does not pretend to offer specific causes for every effect. Instead, it provides the categories like sin and fallenness, the groaning creation, and the plan of redemption that anchor us in reason and revelation instead of absurdity and despair. When I add to my knowledge through a biblical worldview, I don't gain a corner on the next election or an explanation for my child's slow reading capacity. What I gain is a larger frame of reference that replaces my false assumptions with higher and more robust understanding of the way the world works. Hope is impossible if it is not anchored in truth.

The Box-R is a working ranch near Jackson, Wyoming, with a twist. Its guests get to cowboy for real and pay plenty for the privilege. My perceptive wife knew my Western heart and lavished this gift of fantasy cowboying on me.

Each day at the ranch, we rose before dawn, loaded our horses into trailers, and moved herds of cattle to mountain pasture for local ranchers. For thirty-one hours in five days, I was on my high horse. Literally. *Skunk* was my horse for the week: rangy, sure-footed, and tall. He knew cattle, and he showed great patience for his novice rider.

One morning, we split into teams to gather all the cattle from a huge sage-covered range to drive them twelve miles to new pasture. There were four hundred mothers and calves, constantly bawling for each other, having gotten separated in the confusion of the drive. We were driving them about two miles right down the state highway, blocking traffic in both directions. Drivers were patient and understanding, but there was an obvious urgency to get these cattle to a gate and away from the highway.

The little black calves were only two months old. In the confusion of the drive, they lost track of their mamas and listlessly fell to the back of the herd, bawling haplessly, meandering along the fences that bordered the road. One of the calves would occasionally stop, turn around, and begin heading in the opposite direction. He would be instantly mimicked by a dozen others, and before we knew it, we had a jailbreak of bawling, stampeding calves going the wrong way. Skunk and I, and two or three others riding drag, had to head off these panicked calves. With Skunk's speed, it wasn't hard to catch them, but turning them was another story. We waved and whistled and shouted, but it wasn't until some herding dogs were brought back to us that we finally had momentum going in the right direction again. Even then, there were constant attempts by small bunches of calves to turn around. On that day, I learned the value of a good horse and the power of the herd mentality. But I also learned something about hope.

At dinner that night, we suburban cowboys were schooled about what had been happening that morning. Calves only know one thing: stay close to Mama! Their world is exceedingly small. They know Mama by smell, and they depend on her totally for nourishment. Separation from Mama is a calf's worst nightmare, and that's why a moving herd is a cacophony of bawling mothers and calves. As we drove the cattle that day, the calves lost all hope of finding their mothers. But then something dawned on them. They remembered where they had last seen her, and they became desperate to return there to find her again. This is what caused the jailbreak. Desperate loyalty and dependency, without knowledge of the plan or hope for the future, caused a stampede to the past, to safe pasture, to what they once enjoyed.

This is so like the behavior of people. So like me. So like the Israelites after the Red Sea. Add knowledge, admonishes Peter, or, like calves and Israelites, you will grow weary, hopeless, and desperate on the drive to discipleship. Lacking knowledge, we are left to our own reflexes, our own survival strategies. We are hardwired to go back, retreat, give up, and never arrive in a hard-won new place. Only by adding knowledge anchored in biblical peace, life and hope will I be able to keep advancing into faith or goodness, and keep climbing toward self-control, perseverance, brotherly kindness and love.

For personal application:

1. If knowledge doesn't protect me from the afflictions of this world, what good is it?

2. What is the most treasured truth you have come to know about God this year?

3. Have you experienced cognitive dissonance between what you know and the hard things you have experienced?

4. What do you know for sure?

5. What experiences have required a strong handhold on knowledge to keep you from falling?

---

[1] Don Mellor, *Rock Climbing*, (New York, NY, W. W. Norton and Company, 2003), p 13.

[2] Joshua Piven and David Borgenicht, *The Worst-Case Scenario Handbook*, (San Francisco, Ca., 1999)

5

<hr>

Against Gravity

Add to your faith goodness; and to goodness,
knowledge; and to knowledge, *self-control...*

—2 Peter 1:6 (emphasis added)

Handhold #4: Self-control

 Focus! Get hold of yourself. Master your raging emotions. This will not be easy, and there is no one else to rely on. You must marshal all your internal resources because what you do next will determine whether you survive—or not. This was the private monologue of a man whose sole grip on life was his willpower.

Few of us can imagine the command of oneself required of Aron Ralston as he struggled to save his own life. On April 26, 2003, Aron was hiking through Blue John Canyon, a part of Canyonlands National Park in Utah. While he was descending into a narrow, slot canyon, a suspended eight-hundred-pound boulder became dislodged, crushing his right hand against the canyon wall. He forearm was wedged against the wall, which trapped him, and he was unable to move. What was worse, Ralston had not informed anyone of his hiking plans, so he knew no one would be searching for him. Whatever rescue there might be was all up to him. He had to control his panicky thoughts, gather himself together, and do whatever he could.

Assuming that he would probably die in his isolated predicament, he spent five days slowly rationing just twelve ounces of water and two burritos. He tried everything he could think of to extricate his arm, but his efforts proved futile. After three days of trying to lift or break the boulder, the dehydrated and delirious Ralston arrived at the grisly and desperate decision to amputate his trapped right arm at mid-forearm. It was his last and only option for escape. He first experimented with tourniquets and made some exploratory superficial cuts. On the fourth day, he was stymied as he realized that in order to free his arm, he would also have to cut through the bones, but the tools he had available were insufficient to do so.

As he capitulated to his fate, Ralston carved his name, date of birth, and presumed date of death into the sandstone canyon wall and videotaped his last good-byes to his family. He did not expect to survive the night. But after waking at dawn, the following day (Thursday, May 1), he had an epiphany. He could break the radius and ulna bones of his forearm by using his body weight to produce the necessary torque against his trapped arm. He did so, enduring excruciating pain. He then performed the amputation in about an hour with his multi-tool, which included a dull two-inch knife.

He still had several major problems to solve. Ralston still had to get back to his truck. He was weak, dehydrated, and had lost twenty-five percent of his blood. Plus, he had to rappel down a sixty-five-foot sheer wall one-handed and then hike out of the canyon in the hot midday sun. It was eight miles to his vehicle and he had no phone. But while hiking out of the canyon, he encountered a family on vacation from the Netherlands, Eric and Monique Meijer and their son Andy, who gave him Oreos and water and then hurried to alert the authorities. The Meijers proved to be the visible agents of his final rescue, but it was his invisible inner strength and tenacious focus that saved him.[1]

The headline was an attention grabber: "Scientists discover what could be the ultimate workout for couch potatoes: exercise in a pill!" It went on to describe a chemical that had been tested on mice. Mice which were administered the drug but which did not exercise ran forty-four percent farther on a treadmill than mice who did exercise but did not receive the chemical. Just imagine lab-coated scientists trying to measure mouse exercise and nano-technicians designing a Mighty Mouse treadmill. This takes the term *rat race* to a ludicrous new level!

The drug changed the physiology of those mouse muscles, and the developers imagined it would be of great interest to exercise junkies like distance runners, cyclists, and cross-country skiers. However, an unanticipated and unimaginably vast market also looms. Those who never want to break a sweat could now have all the benefits with none of the work! Would this sell or what? Sedentary but image-conscious Americans would love this. I could get the look, the weight, the tone, the health without the time-wasting repetition, the eye-stinging sweat, or the guilt-producing procrastination. Basements and garages now full of rowing machines, ab rollers, and step masters that promised you could look like Christy Brinkley in a week could all be guiltlessly abandoned forever.

If there is any legacy of American inventiveness, from the farm to the kitchen to the office, it is the ubiquity of labor-saving devices. From Cyrus McCormick's first wheat harvester to the iPhone's latest app, we love a quicker, easier way to save ourselves from repetitive labor. For all the benefits this has brought, saving labor has an insidious side effect. We have succeeded in training our expectations to want hard things to be made easy. We want instant "on," instant hot, instant access. We want the heavy to be lifted by someone else or with a hydraulic assist. We want the repetitious to be solved by a smarter machine, harvesting everything in one big swath. We want to add space and activity, but not maintenance. We crave more choices, not greater simplicity. We despise waiting as an affront to our multi-tasking urgency.

Sadly, this pop-tart, microwave attitude influences the ways we pursue our spiritual maturity as well. We can buy any number of spiritual supplements, like this book for example. By doing so, we can certainly learn, but we can also twist instruction into a substitute for exercise, for work, for repetition, or for waiting. We can talk about the subject, have coffee over it, but not actually engage the disciplines. We join, we package, or we reduce complex issues to a five-step formula. None of that old-fashioned grinding it out, slowly progressing in patience, strength or sanctification. There's a new secret. Bypass all those reps. Go from couch to victor's podium instantly! Skip the exercise.

But then our coach Peter, the protégé of Jesus, pedestrian disciple with thirty seasons of experience, shatters the illusion. There will be no performance-enhancing pills for this spiritual journey We will ride the *Tour de France* drug-free. Warning: the road to spiritual ineffectiveness and unproductiveness goes right through the Doritos aisle. If you don't want to leave an epitaph of dissipation, you need to add the sweaty regimen of self-control, and subtract anything that stands between you and a life well-lived.

Hear this necessary discipline as the voice of a mentor, a personal coach who you trust to guide you toward a legacy of personal reward and pragmatic impact on your world. His counsel is priceless, not only because of who he is and how he lived but also because of what his living Master has revealed to him.

Peter deems this handhold of self-control as absolutely essential for our progress in discipleship. Throughout the Scripture, it is incentivized by two powerful, and opposite, motivations: fear and glory. The one is negative and the other is positive. Both are effective.

Fear: The Negative Incentive for Self-Control

Andy was going to make it big. He was salivating over an early retirement, money, and privilege like he had never dreamed he could have, and great generosity to God's work. He had gotten into penny stock trading as a hobby. Each month for several months, he had scored profits in the five-figure range. Now he was all in and taking bigger risks with bigger chunks of money. He guessed wrong. A big gamble folded, and instead of floating into a brilliant future, he found himself face down in huge pit of debt. If he had only known.

The truth is, he had known. At one time, he had proceeded with appropriate caution. He had respected the risk, the exposure. He risked within his margin. He realized there were no guarantees. But with easy success, his appetite took over. Caution was thrown to the wind. He discovered he was the smartest guy in the world. He became addicted to the buzz and lost all fear. Then came the head-on collision with marketplace reality. It would take him years to dig out of the financial chasm that swallowed him whole after his reckless gamble. All for lack of self-control.

There's a feel-good fantasy that all fear is bad for you. Fear is cast as the sadistic and cruel villain in the motivational script. Fear is to be locked away and never allowed onstage. Instead of fear, we are told, every incentive should be positive and uplifting. No Fear on your T-shirt signals you are ready to live large and savor every moment of life. Fear doesn't inspire your best game. Fear should never be used to motivate a child, athlete, or disciple. Fear is the evil carbohydrate in the healthy emotional diet. Stay away from it.

But psychologists tell us that fear of falling is innate. We are born with a stubborn bent toward self-preservation. And if a climber doesn't appropriately fear Isaac Newton's discovery that heavy objects always fall downward with exponential acceleration, he is a fool. Gravity is relentless, and we should properly fear ever becoming that falling object. Gravity isn't just a scientific postulate. It is a blunt-force fact. And if a climber doesn't fear falling, you should fear climbing with him. We can't escape this negative incentive. And self-control is in no small way motivated by fear.

The ancient book of Proverbs spends the first six chapters warning a much-loved son of the pitfalls of neglecting self-control. One particular proverb sears an indelible image into our minds: "Like a city whose walls are broken down is a man who lacks self-control" (Prov. 25:28). The observer portrays not just a city without walls but a formerly walled city whose walls are now destroyed—exposing its inhabitants to the violence and plunder of intruders who have no interest in anybody's welfare. Predators are free to stalk and prey on the innocent. Vandals and flimflam artists are unrestrained by watchmen on the walls. There are no gates to protect the vulnerable nor infrastructures to promote health.

History keeps showing us what a tragedy this is, like Sarajevo during the Bosnian conflict of the 1990s. The simplest daily tasks of life became complex and dangerous. The tragedy of that once thriving, scenic, ancient city being turned into a killing zone was broadcast nightly for many months.

We should contemplate, and fear, this scenario. Fear that builds safeguards to prevent the catastrophic and preserve something valuable is constructive, both collectively and personally. Teaching a child, or anyone, to fear this calamity is not cruel, but wise.

Actor Richard Burton was a superstar a few decades ago whose name is linked to some of Hollywood's biggest blockbusters and to Elizabeth Taylor to whom he was married twice. At the time of his death in August 1984, *Newsweek Magazine* eulogized him:

> *After his sudden death at fifty-eight from a cerebral hemorrhage, there was only one adjective in the headline of the New York Times obituary—'rakish.' Rakish? Is that all that was left of the extravagant gifts of the greatest living actor? It was the blaze of Burton's personality and private life that scorched his laurel crown. Five marriages, a drinking problem that sometimes went public; a yacht-owning, diamond-buying life-style that has been estimated at $80 million worth of consumerism—those took over and turned Burton into an artist who chose desire over discipline.*

Many thought him a genius. He was superior in everything he tried. Handsome, athletic, and unafraid of a fight, yet he also read voluminously and sang beautifully. But, he became split between his appetite for life and

ROGER THOMPSON

discipline for his art. His appetite won. His pursuits of booze, sex, and fame produced only personal isolation and a twisted professional path strewn with cast-off potential.

The words of Peter hang ominously over this epitaph. "Ineffective and unproductive" (2 Pet. 1:8) are the saddest summations of a life that had such great potential but lacked self-control.

An older definition of self-control is "a state untouched by any slumberous or beclouding influence." The self-controlled person is someone who does not lose physical, emotional, or spiritual orientation. He or she is not "beclouded" by the dazzle or tinsel of empty promises and pleasures. The root of this handhold is power and mastery over oneself. It is the vigorous maintenance of perspective and direction when every temptation pulls toward spiritual sloth or the quick fix. Behind every success is the constant awareness of relentless gravity and the fear of falling.

The sad example of Richard Burton is not used to mock his personal tragedy. It is used because this man had so much: every skill, talent, and social advantage. He had what we want for our children. He browsed the mall of life and took anything off the shelf he desired, yet his free fall was inevitable for lack of self-control. "All who hate wisdom love death" (Prov. 8:36).

So, yes, we should fear with a healthy fear the wounds, the disasters, the collateral damage that awaits a life without self-control. It is not an add-on for the few but a requirement for all.

Beware Independence:

Two major warning signs ought to arouse a healthy fear and drive me toward self-control. The first is independence.

Most of the times I have fallen and hurt myself happened because I insisted on doing things my own way, self-assured in my own independent agenda but swathed in ignorance. It's natural. Since Adam and Eve took the first step toward independence from God, this has been the trajectory of every individual. Certain methods and reactions seem obvious to me. Why don't you see it this way? Why read the directions? Why pause to ask someone with experience? Why submit my plans to the team? Why quench my raging appetite? Why slow down when the obvious reward is within my grasp? Why question my gut reactions? My independent analysis and sovereign opinion are airtight. What could possibly go wrong?

The problem with this hubris is not just in the measurable world of decisions and tactics. But loving my independence has a profound influence over my inner reactions, my private assessments, and my character development. Independence makes me distant from, or impervious to, counsel. I drift like an unmoored boat on a sea of whims.

Self-control is an internal discipline that begins in humility. It recognizes that human nature is my nature. I'm the one described in 2 Timothy 3:2–3: "People will be lovers of themselves...without self-control." Did you catch that? Loving myself and lacking self-control are a package deal! Self-assured, self-contained, self-consumed independence is the very definition of lacking self-control. "A fool finds no pleasure in understanding, but delights in airing his own opinions" (Prov. 18:2). A penchant for independence nurtures an aversion to wisdom. Therefore, the first application of self-control is not in the visible world, muscling up disciplined behavior, but in the inner world of understanding and governing self.

How many climbing partners, marriage partners, friends, and colleagues are strewn along the road of life because self-control has not triumphed over stubborn independence to restrain impulses, steer wishes, or guard words? How much money, time, and talent have washed down the storm sewer because there was no channel of self-control to direct their usefulness? Selfishness is not that I want things my way. Selfishness is insisting that you should always want things my way too! Self-control begins by recognizing my own human nature, not with a list of outward rigors. It starts with an internal humility.

Self-control, ironically, doesn't find its center in the self. Its center is located in the humble submission of the self under a greater calling and an indisputable Master. Self-control is looking both ways before crossing the street—every time, despite how important or invulnerable I think I am. It is the submission of my own sovereign opinions to the instruction of the Word, the wisdom of experience, and the conviction of the Holy Spirit.

Self-control keeps humility in play at all times by daily practicing interdependence. Interdependence creates a stronger team and wiser decisions, but it requires much more time and patience. Self-control coaches me to back off my agenda, relax my timeline, and submit my ideas to others. Self-control coaches me to listen to the creative input of colleagues and humbly receive tweaks and changes to directions I once thought unassailable. Self-control opens my ears to suggestions, wise warnings, and a healthful diet. Growing in self-control teaches me to measure my words of rebuttal, time my feedback for maximum effect, and examine my motive before I react to offense. Unchecked independence is nothing more than self-possessed indulgence in the world of me. Humbly fear it, or you will climb alone.

Beware Indulgence:

The second warning sign of a lack of self-control is indulgence. We almost automatically think of the many ways self-control applies to laziness, procrastination, and lethargy, those nasty little attitudes of negligence we allow to pile up and ignore. But there is a more insidious danger, especially in the developed Western world. It's not so much what we fail to do, but what we choose to do that displays our lack of self-control. Suburban America flaunts a candy store of endless options that dazzle the eye, whet the appetite, and promise instant pleasure.

I have a friend who served in Spain as a missionary. He spent his first four years immersed in Spanish culture and language. When he returned on his first home assignment, I asked him, "What strikes you about America after having been away these past four years?"

John answered, "Americans are obsessed!" I asked him to explain. "Americans seem to feel if they can do something, they must pursue it to the ultimate degree." He went on to cite the obsessions of parents to train up an Olympian by hiring a personal coach, moving lock, stock, and barrel to another city, and turning childhood into a workout schedule. He pointed to the fast-tracking of preschoolers, the preoccupation with traveling sports, the families whose every discretionary dollar and hour is spent on achieving, excelling, and practicing. Camps are devoted to skill development. Sports are about practice, not play. Spiritual community, the church, is relegated to the backwaters of priorities slightly ahead of re-organizing one's sock drawer.

John pointed out the compulsive perfectionism portrayed endlessly on the cable channels: perfect woodworking projects flow from extravagantly equipped shops; the finest cuisine emerges effortlessly from the cooking show oven; perfectly toned complexions are regaled by models on infomercials; ten-year-old entrepreneurs are paraded as trophies of successful parenting. America, in his view, had totally lost its moorings to unbridled obsessions. Indulgence has become a way of life.

The frenzied, exhausted, and spiritually anorexic middle class is a textbook case study for the lack of self-control. The slurry of advertising, the green eye of envy, and the instant access to credit renders "enough" an obsolete word. We are easily addicted to innocent things and a plethora of good things. Only self-control will help us exercise the word *no*, or even *slow*.

Avoiding disaster through self-control is simple, but not easy. It is about knowing what is good for you and what isn't. But it's usually not binary. It's not an on-off switch, or a choice between pristine purity and reeking rottenness. It's daily, hourly, basic portion control of my appetite for food, drink, leisure, and success. Self-control learns and practices when enough is enough. But there is not one message from popular culture or media that encourages this. We have been systematically trained not to value self-control because our models of success are examples of obsession, not balance.

Paradoxically, it's mentally and spiritually lazy to be a fanatic. It's easy. All you have to do is abandon balance and strive single-mindedly toward one goal. Our culture gives trophies for fanaticism, obsession, and single-focused me-ism. They are accolades for imbalance, accompanied by the victor's orthodoxy: "Don't ever let anyone stand in the way of your dreams!"

Self-control, whether saying "Enough" at the table, to the television, or limiting the activity options for our families, sounds like a throwback to a previous generation. It sounds as corny as a return to the typewriter or the rotary telephone. It feels like we are opting for irrelevancy in an ever-accelerating culture. But the loving warnings about self-indulgence are timeless. "If you find honey, eat just enough—too much of it, and you will vomit" (Prov. 25:16).

Our children are hurried through childhoods loaded with practice but bereft of play. This is because parents lack self-control, being intimidated by the pressures of perfectionism. Our Sundays are seldom Sabbaths. Corporate worship is too often a turnout on the way to something more important or reduced to a few consecutive Sundays between seasons when game schedules don't interfere. Rest as a part of the Sabbath gift is in a well-documented deficit across all age categories. Debt, discarded toys, hurried childhoods, and fractured marriages tell a bitter tale of our haste toward indulgence. Be afraid, be very afraid, of lacking self-control.

Glory: The Positive Incentive for Self-control

As a collegiate distance runner, I logged many one-hundred-mile weeks with my fellow gaunt teammates. This heavy mileage was to build a base of endurance for the real work ahead. As we sharpened for the fall cross-country season or the spring track season, we began doing dreaded "interval" workouts. These were usually one-lap, quarter-mile repeats at race pace or faster, followed by a rest "interval" of a half lap of jogging. Typically, we did twenty repeats like this. As the season progressed toward bigger meets and championships, our pace got faster, and the rest interval got shorter. After the first one or two intervals our gaggle of shared suffering fell silent. Each man was focused on his own fatigue and pain. It was all we could do to just survive the workout.

Why would anyone do something this hard? Did we find spiritual joy in suffering? Were we just trying to keep from getting fat or avoid heart disease? Were we concerned about cholesterol or bone density later in life? Why would anyone exercise like this? It's simple. It was for the glory. Not the glory of the workout or the admiration of our girlfriends. It was for the glory of the prize we had in mind. We were gunning for a district championship and ultimately a national championship. In light of that quest, getting up early for training runs and bypassing midafternoon snacks were nothing. We joyfully suspended many a desire in order to pursue something we deeply wanted. Because we prized a high goal, we tenaciously aligned our lives with that goal. Self-control was a natural by-product of this greater goal. We were drawn along toward something bigger than ourselves.

Lifelong self-control is all about the goal. Focusing on that greater goal keeps me from chasing every shiny object so that I can achieve my greater purpose and enjoy a deeper satisfaction. Self-control is the natural discipline for pursuing what I really want, not chasing after what I temporarily desire. In the New Testament, the runner, the boxer, the athlete, the farmer, and the soldier are positive examples of self-control. The apostle Paul writes of himself:

> *Everyone who competes in the games goes into strict training. They do it to get a crown that will not last; but we do it to get a crown that will last forever. Therefore I do not run like a man running aimlessly, I do not fight*

like a man beating the air. No I beat my body and make
it my slave so that after I have preached to others, I
myself will not be disqualified for the prize.

—(1 Cor. 9:25–27)

Self-control comes naturally when we see the prize toward which we strive. Paul said he did everything "for the sake of the gospel" (1 Cor. 9:23).

So self-control is not merely a warning barricade to avert catastrophe. It is not a nervous denial of every satisfaction or a loathing of all enjoyment. Nor is it a consignment to mediocrity. On the contrary, self-control is the pathway to excellence and satisfaction but through a different portal than chasing eye candy. The true disciple of his art, his sport, or his Lord is a person who wants the highest, the best, and the most lasting reward. He wants glory, not just a string of experiences. He wants to ascend, not simply keep himself from falling.

One of the most prevalent and vexing addictions for men is the lure of pornography. Available with a couple of clicks of the mouse, a man can be transported toward detached and artificial self-gratification in seconds. Its magnetism is powerful, and its destructive power in marital and spiritual lives is devastating. I don't need to recount here why it should be avoided. But its grip is ferocious and addictive. How does a man free himself from it?

Many approaches emphasize intentional small group accountability and transparency. This is essential and proves to be very helpful. However, unless we are careful, we can fool ourselves into believing that avoiding sin is all that is necessary for the maintenance of purity. It is not. Instead, every man, no matter what his weakness may be, must ask himself, "Where am I going? What is my goal? What do I want to accomplish with this day, this season of marriage, these decades of life?" Unless a man is drawn by a greater *yes*, he will not be sustained by a louder *no*. A man must find something glorious to pursue.

Glory is what we were designed to strive for. Put aside visions of celebrities on the red carpet or ticker-tape parades down Broadway after the Super Bowl. The glory we were designed for is weightier and longer lasting than this glitz. It's a word that speaks of worth, dignity, and gravity. Glory prompts silence and humility, not Twitter posts. Mostly it is applied to God Himself, and His radiance and splendor. Glory is displayed in the created world in the awesomeness of the night sky or the beauty of a double rainbow. These glimpses of glory point us to God. True glory draws us, humbles us, and silences us. Glory puts everything else in perspective. It miniaturizes me, my perspective, and everything in the world.

We crave true glory. True glory takes the itch out of temporary desires. The glory that was once an attribute of humanity became a hungry and elusive quest because we were darkened by sin. Glory was sullied and obscured in Adam and Eve's rebellion and eviction. But the redemptive thread that runs through the Old Testament is tied to the Redeemer Himself, and draws us back to glory. Jesus Christ, in His incarnation revealed God's glory: "The Word became flesh and made his dwelling among us. We have seen his glory, the glory of the One and only, who came from the Father, full of grace and truth" (John 1:14). He completed the work of atonement and brought "glory on earth" (John 17:4).

Ascending toward this glory is the highest calling of the Christ follower. But it is an incremental, daily ascent

coached along by self-control in the most mundane of
details. "So whether you eat or drink or whatever you do,
do it all for the glory of God" (1 Cor. 10:31). Giving up ice
cream is a mere trifle if I do it for the glory of an Olympic
gymnastics gold medal. So, too, is the daily discipline of
self-control practiced in bringing glory to Jesus Christ.
The prospect of His presence, His guidance, and His
commendation shrinks every other desire and disciplines
every daily decision. Just hearing his "well done" is worth
every sacrifice.

Richard lives this. Healthy, mobile, and still working
in his mid-seventies, he is a model of glory-directed self-
control. He recently mentioned that he has bought his last
pair of shoes, his last winter coat, and his last car. It's not
that he is morbid or preoccupied with impending death. He
may well live another fifteen or twenty years. So why such
seeming austerity? He simply doesn't want the distraction
of more stuff. He doesn't need it. More amazingly, he really,
truly, doesn't desire it. When he speaks of this, it is with
a wide smile, not an ascetic scowl. He is freeing himself
from distractions to pursue his assignments to the glory of
God. Care for his wife, his ministry of caregiving to needy
adults, and his constant life of prayer are the quests of his
life. Resoling his old shoes or driving his high-mileage car
is no sacrifice. What appears to be self-denial is actually a
glory-embracing joy. He is pursuing glory. Not his own, but
God's.

Richard shows us how self-control turns theology into
biography. Still, it is not automatic, and the following three
disciplines may help us define and focus our efforts:

1. *Inner self-control*: "Above all else, guard your heart,
   for it is the wellspring of life" (Prov. 4:23). If we learn

anything from Scripture, it is that iron-clad, outward self-discipline will never tame the heart. "The heart is deceitful" (Jer. 17:9), and no one can truly know it except God Himself. Rigid, external legalism retards and restricts but never transforms the heart. It cannot inoculate me against the virus of passion within.

Inner self-control begins fresh every day by submitting in humility to the inspection, repentance, cleansing, and renewal of my wayward heart to my Master. This is deeper and more profound than behavior modification or impulse control. This is wanting the prize, desiring purity, and longing for usefulness enough to practice a distrust of myself and a reliance on God. Self-control flows from the inside out.

2. *Environmental self-control*: I would be a fool indeed if I want to ascend to a summit but pay no attention to my context, my companions, and weather conditions. "Put away perversity from your mouth; keep corrupt talk far from your lips. Let your eyes look straight ahead...Make level paths for your feet and take only ways that are firm. Do not swerve to the right or the left; keep your foot from evil" (Proverbs 4:24–27).

We practice self-control in order to move toward the consequences we want in life. If I want to lose twenty pounds by Labor Day, I will not allow my environment to be stocked with ice cream, Ding Dongs, and chips and dip. If I choose to pursue a vibrant, growing marriage, I will practice speaking wholesome and affirming words to my spouse every day. I will plant seeds of gratitude and refrain from diverting fantasies, flirtatious dalliances, or harbored anger. If I want unity in the body of Christ, I will rid my environment of gossip, limit my time addressing certain topics, and keep a distance from those who stir up strife.

Name your weakness. There is some next right thing you can do to rid your environment of prompters that sabotage your goals and your self-discipline. This chosen austerity is not the essence of self-control, but there will be no self-control at all if stumbling blocks are allowed to clutter your path, and sirens are never placed out of reach. This may be the place to ask if, in your journey of discipleship, you have willingly renounced anything for the sake of your usefulness to the Lord. Do you so long for the glory of the "Well done" from the Master that you joyfully steer yourself around the thicket of diversions and distractions?

3. *Emotional self-control*: Daniel Goleman[2] has highlighted the powerful influence of our EQ, or emotional intelligence quotient. EQ in maintaining healthy relationships in the office or the home is more important than IQ. He describes emotional intelligence as "managing feelings so that they are expressed appropriately and effectively, enabling people to work together smoothly toward their common goals." According to Goleman, the four major skills that make up emotional intelligence are

   - Self-awareness
   - Self-management
   - Social awareness
   - Relationship management

119

This all may sound very corporate and theoretical, but I would suggest that Goleman is simply observing what the New Testament has taught for two thousand years. Ephesians 4:29 is a timeless tutorial on emotional intelligence and the self-control necessary to enjoy relational health: "Do not let any unwholesome talk come out of your mouths, but only what is helpful for building others up according to their needs, that it may benefit those who listen."

A world of emotional self-control is compressed in the next three verses (Eph. 4:30–32). First and foremost, it is practiced to avoid grieving the Holy Spirit who inhabits every believer. It is tutored by the wisdom of the "replacement principle." Self-control is not stalwartly saying no in rigid self-denial. While the disciple does indeed say no to bitterness, rage, and anger, he simultaneously says yes to kindness, compassion, and forgiveness. Emotional self-control aims for the higher goal of unity and love, not the denial of real struggle. Rather, self-control helps me choose to speak to the true need, not just react to the perceived wound.

The next right thing for you might well be the same old right thing that has slipped out of use or fallen into disrepair. Self-control is a handhold we ought to know quite well. Perhaps there is nothing so right for now, so familiar from the past, and so trustworthy for future joy than a firm grip on self-control.

For personal application:

1. How have you learned self-control the hard way—through hurtful consequences?

2. What goal do you pursue which causes you to be self-controlled so that you can attain it?

3. List two or three behaviors or attitudes where more self-control would result in greater strength or effectiveness.

4. What situation have you faced where self-control was the primary handhold to keep you from falling?

---

[1] As told by Aron Ralston, *Between a Rock and a Hard Place*, (New York, NY, Atria Books, 2004)

[2] Daniel Goleman, *Emotional Intelligence* (New York, NY, Bantam Books, 1995)

6

Suffering Well

Add to self-control, perseverance.

—2 Peter 1:7

Handhold #5: Perseverance

 "Trees above timberline have a dimension to their growth not often recognized by the casual passerby. It is the rare and elegant beauty of the actual wood produced with the wind-tossed trees. The grain is of exquisite texture interspersed with whorls and curving lines of unusual gracefulness. The stresses and strains of tossing and twisting in the wind and sleet and deep snows of winter produce an extra flow of resins, giving the tree's fibers a remarkable tight-grained texture and emanating an exquisite fragrance.

An expert violin maker, who is a master craftsman, tells me that he spends weeks each summer searching for special trees above timberline. From these he takes his choicest material to create musical instruments of the finest quality and tone.

Wood produced in the high and tough terrain above the usual timber stands bears within it a rare timbre and lovely resonance not found in ordinary lumber cut at lower elevations. The fury of storms, the shortness of the growing

---

season, the wrenching of the winds, the strain of survival in such an austere setting—all these combine to produce some of the toughest, choicest, most wondrous wood in all the world.

Here is wood grown on a gaunt rock ridge on some remote mountain range that one day will grace a violin, cello, or guitar in Lincoln Center. From those tree fibers will come the finest music ever made by man. Its melodies and notes will enrich a thousand listeners, and, by modern communication, encircle the globe to inspire a million more.

But it all began with a sturdy tree, set apart, growing slowly, unknown, all alone on a distant hill against the sky edge."[1]

The best way to frame the concept of perseverance is to take you on a journey. This specific story may not be your experience, but the lessons from it will connect at some point with your journey. Come along on a bike ride that showed me the value of perseverance, and the innate avoidance we harbor for this virtue.

We were wolfing down our lunch under a cloudless sky at a roadside table in Poncha Springs, Colorado. Not much of a place, but it represented a trip-defining right turn on the map for us. We had pedaled south out of Buena Vista that morning, our second full day on our quest to reach Cortez in the southwest, Four Corners area of Colorado. The trip would take five days, over seven high passes, fueled by Kool-Aid, tuna fish, and peanut butter. Twelve of us had left Denver on bicycles: heavy old Schwinns and Huffys weighing more than thirty pounds.

This was medieval biking. We really didn't know what we were doing, so we pooled our ignorance and concocted what had turned into a fine and pleasant form of misery previously unknown to any of us. We wore cut-off jeans and Converse sneakers. It was 1973, and real bicycle helmets hadn't hit the market yet. So we wore hockey helmets, ironically labeled Cool Gear. Not a stitch of Lycra or padding of any kind adorned our bodies. Cotton T-shirts. We were sore and sunburned. But now we were in too deep to back out. Poncha Springs was our Rubicon. This was the westward turn that would test every commitment we had made to each other. As we gulped our lunch, we couldn't keep our eyes from wandering upward, to the west, to the place we had to ride. The big one loomed. We didn't want to talk about it. Monarch Pass.

The highway undulates through the valley we had ridden that morning, hugging the foothills along the Arkansas River. It was beautiful riding: the river, the fragrance of freshly cut hay in the meadows, and, except for a few challenging hills, an easy pull. The brilliance of the Rocky Mountain sun, the pristine air, and the breathtaking vista, however, could not suppress our unspoken fears. We were turning west toward the spires and crags of the Rocky Mountains. The road led only upward, seventeen miles to the summit of Monarch Pass: elevation 11,312 feet. Four thousand vertical feet of climbing against the gravity of both body and soul.

These teenagers had been full of surprises. Adult and child, athlete and whiner, comedian and mutineer were stirred together in a volatile mix. They were exasperating, resilient, demanding, altruistic, childish, selfish, and tough. This day they were inspiring. Knowing full well that there was no way to soften the reality of at least three hours of six percent, uphill, first-gear grinding to reach the top, they set out with dogged, sunburned determination. Four thousand feet had to be climbed with leg, lung, and will power alone. With a wide range of motivations and abilities, they were soon sorted into clusters of fellow survivors. Gasping, hunched, and glassy-eyed, they fixed their stares at the pavement just in front of their tires as the pass rose relentlessly upward. "Snail's pace" acquired a working definition on that afternoon. But they did it! Eventually everybody summited. They amazed themselves and cheered victory to each other at the top. For most, this was the pinnacle of any physical challenge they had ever attempted. There was a high-five celebration when the caboose finally arrived and a glow of utter satisfaction on every face. Brownies were awarded as the ultimate payoff for their courage. As we flew down the western side of the pass, the hoots and cheers never stopped.

Fresh off that victory, we spurred one another on and rode a hundred miles the next day into Montrose. When I think back on our inexperience, our ludicrous attire, and our greenhorn unpreparedness, it is utterly audacious that we even tried this, much less accomplished it. Time after time, we met people at rest stops and mountain summits who asked, "How did y'all get here?" When we replied that we had ridden our bikes from Denver, they were a study in ambivalence. Were we lying—or crazy? Their dropped-jaw amazement just fueled our team with more determination.

But we weren't done. We still had huge, looming challenges on our horizon. We were headed into the "Switzerland of America" and its legendary "Million Dollar Highway." The fourth day would take us to Red Mountain Pass, 11,008 feet in elevation. From the Swiss-like village of Ouray, the pass looks endless and dangerous. No guard rails. The Million Dollar Highway is cut into the steep scree slopes the color of rusting iron. A lapse of concentration or a lane-hogging flatlander behind the wheel of an RV and a cyclist would be gravely injured. But the group was becoming resolute. We were eager to grind it out, to tackle the pass. Again, we left river and meadow, and finally, timberline, behind. We summited and celebrated after 3,500 feet of vertical gain. We posed for a victory picture and then broke the sound barrier on our descent.

This gaggle had melded into a real team. We had learned how to encourage one another. We fixed flats and kept moving. We sang and joked and teased. Our unity was hard won from the agonies of climbing, camping, freezing, and burning together. As we cruised down this final pass, following the Purgatory River into Durango, we were Lance Armstrong. We were the Tour de France. We were indefatigable. Celebration time. Chocolate shakes all around. All our passes were behind us. Now, all that remained was a forty-mile cruise into Cortez, a victory lap of sorts, our Champs-Elysees.

The mistake we made was to ask an out-of-state tourist who had driven into Durango from the West what we could expect of the road ahead. "Oh, it's mostly level," he said. "Probably downhill, slightly rolling, in the direction you're going. Easy traveling..." He set our expectations on coasting and cruising and sowed the seeds of our inglorious demise.

Assumptions were made and frozen into place. Expectations were set by that innocent but erroneous description of the road ahead. We were soon to discover that when the assumption is the enjoyment of a downhill cruise with little exertion, then every uphill becomes an insult, a personal and painful affront. The offense fueled anger that had to be vented somehow. Our resilient and intrepid team rapidly fragmented into an epithet-spitting mutiny.

Leaving Durango, we began to climb, completely contrary to our assumptions. We climbed and we climbed.

It was hot and dry, and our sunburned necks were being fried. The hill wouldn't end. This wasn't the plan. It wasn't supposed to be this way. It isn't fair! The irresistible force of expectation ran headlong into the immovable object of reality. Seething frustration boiled up from the senseless suffering. The breathless heat blotted out all memory of mountain highs and victory pictures. Who planned this trip? This is stupid! I'm quitting! You leaders are morons!

Expectations are stubborn things. Once fixed in our minds, they become our axis, the center of our universe. Every experience is sucked into the gravitational field of these expectations. And if our experience does not line up and neatly orbit around our expectations, we want to hurl this reality into outer darkness. We want our universe to run as expected, on demand. On this day, in this heat, under these unanticipated adversities, there was such an explosion of blame, anger, and rejection that our whole universe was stunned into a cosmic funk. Our team disintegrated into isolated planets of misery.

This motley team erupted in a toxic cataclysm of blame, selfishness, and spitefulness. Mutiny was in full swing. We were on the verge of mayhem, and murder was whispered. Gone was any memory of sweet teamwork. One brazen fact was stubbornly resisted: it was still an uphill climb and nobody was going to climb it for us. The next right thing, the next pedal revolution, was the least favorite option.

Don't be surprised:

Scott Peck once began a book with this statement of biting realism: "Life is difficult. Most do not fully see this truth that life is difficult. Instead they moan more or less incessantly, noisily or subtly, about the enormity of their problems, their burdens, and their difficulties as if life were generally easy, as if life should be easy."[2] Whether he knew it or not, his thoughts echoed those of the apostle Peter, who nineteen hundred years beforehand declared, "Dear friend, do not be surprised at the painful trial you are suffering as though something strange were happening to you" (1 Pet. 4:12). Peter is the man who now coaches us with the next right thing in his array of life skills.

So what does this brilliant life coach suggest for the weary slogger, the frustrated, angry, or disenfranchised victim? "Perseverance," says Peter, is the next right thing for many whose journey seems endlessly uphill. But we would rather hear of some other way. Can't I quit, or catch a magical ride, or simmer in an angry snit instead? Can't I shift the blame onto someone else? Wouldn't anything be better than to be coached to persevere? Persevere in the same old routine, through the same level of pain, with the same old cast of characters? Yes, this *least* favorite thing is the next right thing given to us through the divine power and wisdom of the Father, because He knew we would need it in this uphill, sun-scorched world (2 Pet. 1:3).

Perseverance needs careful definition. We need to split a semantic hair to distinguish its nuance from another word often used as a synonym: *endurance*. Our Rocky Mountain bikers had demonstrated endurance repeatedly. What they had yet to embrace on that maddening hill west of Durango was perseverance. The difference is huge. These novice cyclists had endured much. They had shown tenacity, a capacity to suffer, and a growing tolerance for delayed gratification. By the time they reached Durango, they had ridden three-hundred and fifty miles, awakened in soggy tents, and broken ice from their bicycle seats in Silverton. They had spent eight hours per day in the saddle enduring the hassle of waiting for slowpokes, and the unavoidable grunge of sweat and camping. They endured.

But right there is the important distinction between endurance and perseverance. Each day they endured because they could see a finish line or a series of achievable goals. They were promised an end at the next rest stop, town, summit, or campsite. Despite their suffering, they knew there would be an end and some modicum of reward, so they admirably endured.

Perseverance is different:

Perseverance has a different, but important twist. Though perseverance requires the same expensive and exhausting expenditure of energy, the same exertion against inertia, it lacks that one shimmering appeal: a finish line. Perseverance lacks an end, or at least, a known end. Perseverance is a steady persistence, a courageous fortitude, a doggedness with a very disturbing caveat: the finish line is not known, or it is unseen and lying on the far side of a daunting and ugly hill. Perseverance is that courage that presses on when the end is not what we envisioned, or what we wanted.

Endurance is running the mile.
Perseverance is running a household.
Endurance is learning Algebra.
Perseverance is learning to live with diabetes.
Endurance is rehabbing after knee surgery.
Perseverance is starting life again after divorce.
Endurance is winning eight Olympic gold medals.
Perseverance is living with two preschoolers in the house.

Endurance is hard.

Perseverance seems unfair.

Because we live in a culture of sound bites and "extreme makeover," it is easy to slip into the assumption that somebody somewhere has a magical solution. Add to this the formula mill of well-meaning friends proposing solutions and the conclusion is that perseverance must be only for those who can't step into their spiritual victory. But it turns out, and the apostle Peter affirms, that much of life can be met only with the next right thing called perseverance. But sometimes this seems like the least spiritual of all the options.

Brent and Sarah exude a magnanimous spirit from every pore of their lives and every word from their mouths. How wonderfully he encourages and how insightfully she teaches. Their legacy will be one of self-giving servanthood and humble faithfulness. They are truly the pillars, bastions of grace, of which any healthy church is built. But unseen by many, they must relentlessly carry huge weights that sap their energies and remove them from circulation. They give days of each week to care for a grandson whose father is MIA. Sarah continues in a high-stress job despite a heart functioning at sixty percent. Aging parents and extended family, most of whom live locally, require constant expenditures of free time, holiday plans, and vacation days.

They have endured uncountable laps of this long run, and there is no end in sight. When they do have moments to ponder and project into the future, they see no changes. In fact, they see only deeper risk, more complications, and further erosion of health and resources. Each day as they awaken to work, grandparenting, needs of extended family, and financial austerity, they are met with the only choice they have. It is their best choice, but their least pleasant choice to live a God-honoring life: they choose to persevere. Where's the downhill coasting, or the ultimate victory, in that?

Our coach, Peter, in his list of life-defining skills (2 Pet. 1:5–8) makes a logical sandwich with perseverance as its meat. This chewy, tough, dogged form of endurance is sandwiched between self-control and godliness. The private battles against anger, retreat, self-gratification, and vengeance won with self-control, usher in the longer war against inertia and despair fueled by perseverance. This, then, creates a character of humility and inward piety which displays authentic godliness in the real world. Self-control links to godliness through the fibrous connective tissue called perseverance.

Author Tim Hansel defines perseverance as "courage stretched out." Consistent courage builds a bridge to obedience with girders of perseverance. Life in this real world must bear the weight of hassle, suffering, and unfairness in order to span to the shore of godliness. Perseverance is what this bridge is made of. It stands without fanfare. The traffic of our lives, and the lives of others, flows across it.

Perseverance bears the weight of challenging and heavy life and makes the commerce between personal faith and public witness flow without interruption. But it is a strain. It requires strength. And there is no end in sight.

Many friends flash across my mind whose perseverance is epic but unheralded. They are head down, in low gear, and struggling to keep ascending. Words like *recurring*, *chronic*, *persistent*, *senseless*, *unfair*, and *unexpected* dominate their daily experience. They are being squeezed economically in the vice of family needs and a downsizing industry, tested to their limits every day by special needs children, made frantic over grandchildren facing chemotherapy, and pouring fading hope into a marginal business or an eroding marriage. The way ahead looks hard, and the end they see is neither pretty nor pleasant. Formulas for success seem designed for a different world than theirs. They slog on and have no other option. They groan along with the groaning creation described in Romans 8. Though their conditions are undesirable and harsh, they have made a choice to suffer well, recurringly. They have chosen perseverance with self-control and have not insisted that somebody somewhere owes them a free ride.

We may choose to suffer well, with perseverance, or we can seethe in despair about the unfairness of a universe turned against us. The next best thing about the Bible, besides its crescendo of victory, resurrection, and redemption, is its utter clarity and truth telling regarding trouble on a groaning planet. Trouble is not grudgingly acknowledged. It is headlined on every page of Scripture. Jesus took away any pretense when he asserted, "In this world, you will have trouble" (John 16:33). Paul makes a theological blanket statement, leaving no one immune, or insulated, from distress: "We know that the whole creation has been groaning as in the pains of childbirth right up to the present time. Not only so, but we ourselves, who have the firstfruits of the Spirit, groan inwardly as we wait eagerly for our adoption as sons, the redemption of our bodies" (Rom. 8:22–23).

Those of us with a biblical worldview should not be surprised when trouble comes. But moderns, even believers, surviving on quick-fix assurances of easy victory, fed by the chip-and-dip empty calories of the media, find it hard to chew on the gristle of perseverance. But there it is, immediately following Hebrews 11, the stirring chapter documenting the great triumphs of faith.

> *Therefore, since we are surrounded by such a great cloud of witnesses, let us throw off everything that hinders and the sin that so easily entangles, and let us run with perseverance the race marked out for us. Let us fix our eyes on Jesus, the author and perfecter of our faith, who for the joy set before him endured the cross, scorning its shame, and sat down at the right hand of the throne of God.* (Heb. 12:1–2)

This high-strength piton of perseverance is driven into the rock of Jesus' example and the Father's faithfulness. Our whole life hangs on it. *Hupomeno* is the Greek compound word. It welds two concepts together: bearing up, and under. The visual picture is that of bearing up under, remaining true under pressure. Despite the pain, disappointment, or fearsome potential, perseverance hangs on to what it knows, to whom it trusts. After the inspiration gained from the gallery of faith in Hebrews 11, the first word of counsel in Hebrews 12 about living life today recommends the brawny handhold of perseverance.

Maybe we should think more personally, more practically. Is perseverance the next right thing for me right now? Is there an unwanted, unexpected, and deeply disliked circumstance looming before me, or already upon me? It's unfair. Chronic. Daily. Painful. Embarrassing. Unforeseen. It won't lie down, and it won't go away. Blame and ranting have not succeeded in making it stop. Prayers for deliverance seem to go unanswered. It appears to be my inescapable burden. It is the climb that I, and I alone, must make. Will I suffer well, or fume, blame, demand, and vacillate in wasteful frustration?

A lesser grace?

But before we can make a redemptive choice to persevere as the next right thing, we need to defang a debilitating lie about its value. Perseverance, in contrast to victory stories, and health-and-wealth formulas, is made to appear as one of God's lesser (much lesser) graces. In the shadow of hundreds of pain-relieving regimens, perseverance seems the fallback option for the remedial, the not-quite bright. In fact, faithful Christ followers who persevere procedure after procedure, biopsy after biopsy, month after month, often feel that they are failing. Or worse, God has failed. Perseverance is the spiritual default status for those who are too dense or disobedient to achieve victory or escape. Perseverance, it seems, is what you get when your faith, your mind, or your will is weak.

So, along with trouble, we often travel with Job's counselors, both externally and internally. Friends don't often encourage perseverance as a grace but only as a fallback option. "Hang in there!" is the street-version bromide tossed over the shoulder as they leave the hospital room. It's a way to change the conversation, because to hang with us in the endless round of perseverance is too ambiguous and discomforting. As with Job, well-meaning friends packing answers counsel almost anything except sheer dogged endurance for the day ahead.

What can be said as an answer, or as a key to victory, to the couple whose seventeen-year-old son is as rigid as a log from an unnamed neuromuscular disease? He now weighs more than his mother, and his needs are 24-7. Every medical intervention has been tried. Home care is needed. Countless emergencies have roused them at night. Medical bills, bottomless bureaucracy, and mind-numbing fatigue consume their days. When can they ever rest, or go out on a date? What is their future? Where, or where, is the finish line?

We need a transformed understanding of this castoff virtue called perseverance, a reissuing of a resource too seldom valued, and too quickly disdained. It is neither a shame nor a lesser grace to persevere. It is not somehow sub-Christian to hang in there with recurring courage, even when it has been months, or years, since the last high-five.

Peter not only writes of this, he lived it. One could posit that Peter's whole apostolic career was one long triathlon of perseverance. Few of us would want to know what he knew from the very beginning of his preaching, coaching ministry. Peter was given irrefutable knowledge from Jesus Himself at his commissioning that he would be waging a war of diminishing returns, culminating in death. From a human, physical perspective, there would be no spectacular ascension, as with Elijah, no peaceful retirement lecture circuit, no university tenure, no stirring, heroic martyrdom. When Peter was recommissioned by Jesus to "feed my sheep," he was also shown how his life would end. *When you are old, you will stretch out your hands, and someone else will dress you and lead you where you do not want to go...Follow me!* (John 21:18–19).

One can only imagine the breathtaking impact of these words on Peter. Spontaneous, powerful, manly, adventurous, independent, and courageous Peter would end his life in helplessness. His physical body would either be impaired from weakness or restrained by fetters. His ready will and loyal heart would be overridden by the will and power of others. He would be forced to go where he did not want to go. John informs us that Jesus showed him his end *to indicate the kind of death by which Peter would glorify God.*

Upon hearing this, two blows must have landed simultaneously on Peter's heart: the first is that he would die as an old man, weak and helpless. The promised kingdom ushered in with trumpets, angels, justice, and fire would not come in Peter's lifetime. Israel would not be liberated. Bad guys would not meet their judge. History would not crescendo under the thunder of Peter's preaching, no matter where, or with what power, he proclaimed the Gospel. There would be no final summit, historically speaking, for Peter to celebrate. He was not ascending to a spectacular, definable victory.

The second blow from this news must have been that it would be by his death that Peter would bring glory to God. His gifts, his organizational skill, his homiletic eloquence— none of these would be the benchmark of glory. Rather, it would be his death, ignominious and unwilling, perhaps untimely, from a human perspective. This seemingly senseless final straightjacket of inability would be terminal. What a prospect to ponder for your remaining years! Yet Peter, knowing full well that he would never enjoy the summit of comfort, fame, national liberation, or peace, put his heart and life on the line every day and persevered.

We need perseverance, it seems, not only because we want to survive but because no matter how slowly we are moving or how weakly we are following, others are watching and drafting off our obedience. As with Peter, perseverance, though not glorious to the practitioner, is immensely glorifying to the Master. Perseverance practiced and embraced is a grace observed for every other fellow struggler. The perseverer validates the core theology of the fall and the need for outside intervention. Perseverance speaks truth in slogging, just as gratitude shouts truth in victory. The Master is in view, and He is glorified.

Peter followed, even when he was in possession of terrible knowledge. The uphill would never end. He would never coast into meadows of ease. He would not meet his end with a sound track, the rapture, a chariot of fire, or on a victory stand. Here we find Peter, writing some thirty years later, coaching a new generation of believers to accept the assignment God is giving to them, both individually and collectively. Echoing in his ears were the words of Jesus, when Peter wanted to know if his assignment was fair and equitable with the task and circumstances placed on others: "What is that to you? You must follow me" (John 21:22).

Truth be known, some of us have resisted the development of perseverance in our array of life skills because we insist on knowing the outcomes first. We demand full disclosure, not only of our risks and benefits but of the very mind of the Master. We want full and comprehensive disclosure of what this exercise will do for us, what it will gain, how it will affect our future, before we approve the Master's plan. We feel entitled to the blessings and privileges of others, the joys and perks of a friend, the notoriety or platform of a contemporary, rather than humble acceptance of our own assignment. But true perseverance listens to the call, receives the sometimes hard facts, and follows. Perseverance bears the name with hope, humility, and expectancy. How we need this tough grace in a culture laced with narcissism and flat denial of brute facts. But there is a more practical, earthy reason we need to develop perseverance.

There are fourteen mountain summits above eight thousand meters (twenty-six thousand feet)—the "death zone." They have legendary names like Everest, K2, Cho Oyo, Llotse, Makalu, and Annapurna. Above twenty-six thousand feet all humans rapidly degrade and will eventually die due to diminished oxygen. Though many have summited without oxygen, every climber knows that, once reaching these stratospheric climes, they are racing the clock.

They must push to a high camp from which to launch a final assault. Then, usually very early in the morning, perhaps 2:00 or 3:00 a.m., they make their final assault on the summit. They must summit and get back down as quickly as possible.

It is a well-known, dark reality of climbing that most mountaineers do well on the ascent; they are focused on the goal and enduring of the suffering. But, tragically, many die on the way down. The descent is the most dangerous part of the climb, both physically and mentally. The body is exhausted, and the mind is cloudy. Psychologically, the thrill is over. The goal has been reached. The summit registry has been signed, and the pictures have been taken.

It is on the descent that a very critical shift in thinking and acting must take place. The climber, who has been choosing and willing, and enduring the upward pursuit of the summit, with all its measurable glory, must now shift his attention and focus to just getting back to the tent. One careful foot plant in front of another. Don't stumble. Don't stub your crampon. Concentrate on the next step, the safe belay, proper hydration, and staying warm. What was a once a gauzy quest is now a migraine. What was once a vision is now altitude sickness. Heroism has been reduced to simply not sitting down, not quitting, and not dying.

This is perseverance. It gets us to the next safe step, the next gasp of oxygen, and the next minimal, incremental stage. Perseverance values the descent, with its routinized checklist, and concerns for basics. This is not glory yet. It's basic survival for now. But unless we learn perseverance in the fog of fatigue and fear, we will not arrive at the next tent, with its hot cup of tea and cadre of fellow strugglers. Though no one can persevere for us, there are many who are like us and who will join us.

Googling "get rich," there are thirty-nine million references available in .17 seconds. For "get well," there were 202 million references in just .18 seconds. "Be successful" netted sixty-five million possibilities in .5 seconds. These are samples of the raging desire we all have for a fix, a bailout, a pill, a sweat-less nirvana on earth. Our life coach Peter would have loved that too. But he loved his Lord and Master more than he craved instant answers. And so Peter gives us a handhold none of us want but all of us need. Persevere. It is the next right thing for today, and most likely, for tomorrow.

For personal application:

1. What challenge do you face right now where there is no end in sight?

2. Have you experienced the gracious encouragement of God as you have persevered?

3. What kind of encouragement can we give to someone who is persevering through an unending trial?

4. How does perseverance differ from fatalism?

5. How have you clung to this handhold when there was no other option?

---

1 Philip Keller, *Sky Edge: Mountaintop Meditations*, (Grand Rapids, Mich., Kregel Publications) pp 85–86

2 Scott Peck, *The Road Less Traveled*, (New York, NY, Simon and Schuster, 1978) p 15

7

A Look in the Mirror

And to self-control, godliness.

—2 Peter 1:7

Handhold #6: Godliness

 Somewhere in Charleston, South Carolina, a deeply embittered twenty-one-year-old murderer sulks in a dark prison cell. He had hoped to incite a new race war by going on a bloody rampage at the Emanuel African Methodist Episcopal Church. Feigning the most despicable form of curiosity, he dropped in as a stranger to a prayer meeting of the faithful. For more than an hour, he sat, listened, and received welcome from those gathered. Then he opened his backpack and mercilessly shot and killed nine of these innocent, peace-giving people.

But instead of sparking a race war, Dylann "Roof's unprovoked violence became the occasion for unexpected grace. Something stronger than hate swallowed up this unspeakable crime. It was forgiveness. It was unadulterated Christianity. It became a showcase for Christlikeness broadcast to a spellbound nation on the evening news.

At his bond hearing, the shooter was addressed by the loved ones of his victims. It would have seemed entirely justifiable for them to lash out at him in rage and bitterness. Instead, one by one, through sobs of grief and tears of pain, they offered him the inexplicable: grace and forgiveness. "I will never be able to hold her again," said one daughter about her murdered mother, "but I forgive you." This was unbelievable mercy and compassion for Dylann Roof the person, and for his soul, in the face of his villainous plot and homicidal rampage.

Columnist Michael Gerson summed it up. "The killer set out to defile a sacred place and ended up showing why it is sacred. These victims and their families have shown what it means to be followers of Christ."

I rounded the corner and bumped face-to-face into a confused-looking, pale, and nearly naked man. It was an extremely awkward moment as we locked eyes and stared at each other. Both of us made clumsy moves to get out of each other's way. But every time I moved, he moved with me. He was clearly embarrassed and eager to get away. I tried to avert my eyes from staring. But the more I moved, the closer he got. We both kept stumbling closer together, pulled by some unseen, magnetic force. This weird, slow-motion choreography lasted only seconds until I realized that I had bumped into myself!

I was using a guest pass to a health club, a state-of-the-art facility. I was fighting a cold, and it was howling winter outside. So, I had taken advantage of the steam room to clear my sinuses. About fifteen minutes in that steamy heat was all I could endure, and I emerged back into the locker room. That's when it happened. I hadn't noticed coming in that almost everywhere you turned in that locker room you were confronted with yourself in floor-to-ceiling mirrors. In this case, it was my head-to-toe, mostly unclad self. It was less than flattering. The person in the mirror did not match the image of myself that I carried in my head. It bore no resemblance to me on my best day, or at least the best day I had frozen in my mind's eye. But I could not dispute what I saw. The mirror wasn't lying. It was doing its job by showing me the perfect reflection of my true self at that moment.

It's a profoundly disturbing and humbling experience to stare at your full-length physical body under harsh fluorescent lights. Have you experienced this recently? You instantly notice things about yourself that can be kept mostly hidden or camouflaged under clothing most of the time. (For the record, I think that's a good practice.) But walking toward that mirror or standing in front of it, you are all there in all your glory—or not. Muscle groups, long ignored, are seen to be in obvious need of attention. Some muscle groups have disappeared entirely! Gravity has been taking its toll. Height and weight proportions are on display. Top, middle, and bottom are there for inspection. Signs of aging, hair loss, and skin tone are undeniable.

I'm sure there is a marketing strategy behind the use of these locker room mirrors. On the one hand, the mirrors feed our craven narcissism. We can't resist looking at ourselves. However, I cynically think the health club management wants to constantly remind me how much work remains to be done. Those mirrors are deliberately placed and well-lit to be as unflattering as possible! Everybody—and I mean everybody—will find something flawed or disproportionate when staring at an accurate reflection of himself or herself. Message received: don't ever let that membership lapse. There's plenty of work yet to do. All that exercise has not yet transformed your body. You haven't reached your goal yet. Don't miss a day. Get a personal trainer. You've let things slide for too long! Keep working!

Of course, for some, these mirrors may backfire and provide the ultimate disincentive. The image people see on each visit to the health club may be so discouraging, or so unimproved after all that sweating, that they give up. It's just too big a mountain to climb. Too much weight to lose. There is too much pain in remembering better, younger, healthier days. No matter how hard they work, it's never going to be that way again. Quitting is the lesser of the pains. Why be confronted on each visit with so much imperfection, so much impossibility?

This kind of full-length, truth-revealing mirror confronts us when Peter points to our next handhold. Look at your reflection in the mirror of *godliness*. That word stops me in my tracks. Suddenly I want dimmer light, a smaller mirror, or more clothes to hide my imperfections. This word causes instant discomfort, because I see clearly that I'm not what I want to be or ought to be. I can't ignore that I am unfinished. I'm not in proportion. I'm not the picture of completeness and spiritual fitness I had imagined myself to be or worked so hard to become. And isn't it inspired and appropriate that right here, inserted into a string of skills and tools that could cause me to feel all muscular, self-reliant, and fit, that I must stop and take a long, naked look into this revealing mirror.

Faith is where we started. From there, Peter has prescribed a spiritual regimen that includes goodness, knowledge, self-control, and perseverance. These are robust strengthening exercises and healthy disciplines. They add to our resilience and stamina in every way. They require work and discipline in cooperation with God's initiative toward us, but we can begin to see some progress. When we practice them regularly, however, we can begin to rely on them as links in a chain of self-mastery—sweaty accomplishments that show that we are indeed Army Strong, the real deal, the go-to guy. Our spiritual walk can so subtly be transformed into a self-congratulatory workout schedule, an Olympian regimen of disciplines instead of a journey of humble faith, We can be diverted into seeing our progress as a source of preening and pride. I can start to look at my image of myself as the standard everyone else should strive to achieve. Comparison and judgmentalism follow. But when we look into the mirror of godliness, we see again who we really are. We are inevitably humbled by the complete picture, the disproportion, the weaknesses, the vulnerabilities, and the amount of work left to do. We are reminded that what began with God's grace and initiative will bear fruit only through humble dependence on God's grace and initiative, because taken as I really am, I'm not much.

Take a good look:

I can almost see the kind eyes of Peter as he pulls us aside from the exercise machines and barbells to a quiet huddle of counsel. It's as if he is saying, "Now that you are learning something about the exertions and healthy disciplines that will make you strong, it is important to remember who you are. Take a look in the mirror." This honest look is not meant for our deflation but for our protection. When we supplement our faith with godliness, we are choosing to remember that subjective confidence and impressive accomplishments are not the goal of this adventure. Nor will they erase the dangers inherent in the climb. Staring into godliness causes me to see again who I really am.

Following Jesus is not just signing up for a course on mastering your future or a pep talk on effective habits. Instead, the effective and productive life is infused with something otherworldly, something not generated by competence or practice. Adding godliness to my repertoire of spiritual exercises resets all my subjective and circumstantial measurements of strength. Staring into this mirror shows me my incompletion and brings me into a consistent posture of humble dependence on someone else. Peter places it into the routine so that it confronts us every day. Without godliness, I am just fooling myself about my spiritual prowess, oblivious of my real vulnerabilities and gaps.

But first we need to know what godliness is, the purpose this mirror serves, and why Peter has placed it here in this string of spiritual handholds. The word translated "godliness" comes from the original Greek word *eusebeia*, which is a compound of two words: well + worship. Well worshiping, or worshiping well, does not depict merely an energetic and well-crafted hour on Sunday morning at church. Rather, *eusebeia* portrays a comprehensive mind-set that is conscious of God's presence in every context we enter. Older traditions would call it piety. It is the daily practice of ascribing worth to the proper object, and the dethroning of all pretenders who would usurp God's singular worthiness. Godliness is not a perfectionistic godlikeness, as if we could achieve supernatural heights of righteousness on our own. It is God-liness, a likeness or reflection in our lives that looks something like the Master we serve. That the image we portray is not perfect is actually Peter's point. Looking at ourselves in the accurate reflection of godliness grounds us regularly in a deep and recurring humility. This is a core discipline for our faith journey: to stand before the mirror and see ourselves accurately.

In climbing terms, the practice of godliness reminds us that we are always "On belay!" Almost the first lesson in climbing safety is how to tie on to another who will hold you and keep you from injuring yourself in a fall. It's a standard and reflexive practice of humility and a recurring nod to harsh reality. To be on belay is the essence of pragmatism! The belay guards you from plummeting to your harm or death. But it also reduces the fear that darkens the challenge ahead.

As a neophyte climber, you are taught that the rope from above must be securely knotted into your climbing harness. You are taught to shout "On belay!" This signals that you want and need the person above you to keep you from falling. You trust him. You need him. You are dependent for your security on his vigilance. It's a humble recognition that this climb will not be accomplished alone and that you are dependent enough to need and welcome help. This dependency is never outgrown.

Even so, some amazing climbers dismiss the need for a belay. They are self-assured purists who want no assistance while scaling some very impressive walls. I watched a YouTube video of an extreme climber named Dan Osman with stomach-knotting tension. He is a "free climber," meaning that he climbs with no ropes or protection. He climbs alone with only his strength, grip, and wits, and no belay. I watched as he almost leapt up a thousand-foot face in Yosemite in less than two minutes. His moves were catlike, quick, decisive, simple, and strong. Everything appeared easy, as if he were working out in a gym. But frequently, the camera would pan back to show the exposure that increased as he climbed higher. It was breathtaking, even on video. One mistake and his life would be over. No belay could save him. As he summited, he was hardly more winded than if he had cruised to the grocery store on his bike. I was both sickened by the cavalier risks he took and fascinated by the incredible skill he displayed. I was captivated, so I surfed the net to find more videos. There were many. Each one recorded his amazing feats and reckless courage. Then, I came upon the video entitled "The late extreme climber Dan Osman." I didn't need to watch any more.

In his book *Rock Climbing*, author and climber Don Mellor warns[1],

> "Rock climbing is a technical sport. Practicing it safely depends on employing the correct techniques, deploying the right gear for the conditions, and tying sequences of complicated knots flawlessly. If you make errors on any of these fronts, serious injury or death could result. Climbers who have had long safe careers are alive today because they understand the risks and behave accordingly, not because they are lucky."

Climbing Magazine lists fifty common mistakes climbers can make. At the very top, number one, is, "Not double-checking your belay and knots." You can never assume.

You must double-check every knot. Is it tied correctly? Is it tightened? Is it threaded through the harness correctly? This inspection is never irrelevant. In 2007, Lara Kellog, an experienced mountaineer, omitted this essential safety precaution. She rappelled off the end of her rope while descending Mount Wake in Alaska. She was killed, falling about one thousand feet. Humble, systematic inspection is never redundant. It is routinely life-sustaining!

Godliness means that we never cease to acknowledge our need for help, strength, and security from another. Godliness is the sober, but routine, practice of being "on belay" with no illusions about our vulnerability in the face of relentless gravity.

So what does godliness look like? Is it a stiff uptightness that looks weird and perpetually out of sync in the office culture? Is godliness next to cleanliness, perfectionism, and honor roll grades? Is godliness recognizable by speaking a religious dialect using words like *blessing*, *glory*, or *hallelujah*? Does godliness major in withdrawal, protest, or moral outrage at our cultural decay? What are the attributes or litmus tests that seem to define *godliness* in your church or spiritual heritage?

Here's a little exercise that gave me an instant grasp of what the practice of godliness might look like in daily life. What one preoccupation would show my total commitment to the advancement of myself? In a word, it would be "Roger-liness." If I make Roger-liness my focus, every other relationship and activity becomes a means to my own self-advancement or reputation. The goal of every seeming virtue is really the honor of me. Roger-liness as a focus puts Roger at the center, Roger at the edges, and too much of Roger in the middle of everything. Everyone around me soon knows my true goals and the axis around which all my energies turn. I am full of myself.

If, on the other hand, I put someone else's name in the blank, an entirely different tone and outcome results. Let's say that my anniversary is approaching and that I, for once, don't want to just grab a gift card from Crate and Barrel to check it off my list. Let's imagine that I really want to honor my wife for who she is and what she has meant to

151

me. I want her to know that I am in debt to her love and kindness and that I cherish her person and her gifts? How could I express that better than by taking on an attitude of "Joanne-liness." For forty-eight hours, I put Joanne at the center of my thoughts, my plans, and my words. I tell her about it. I ask her how I could become better at it. I become "Joanne-ly," meaning that I remember how important she is and has been for every aspect of my life. I say and do the words and deeds most valued by her. I joyously reflect on how my life has been made possible through her love and sacrifice. I drive with her in mind. I come home thinking of her. At work, I remember that I am serving her needs. I gladly provide for her. I talk about her character with others and extol her strengths and talents. Everybody around me gets the point: I am a man who is "Joanne-ly." And would not Joanne be delighted to be at the center of my focused affections and attention?

Now expand this concept to your relationship with God. When we live to give honor and worth to someone else, it shows. It's an inner attitude that sparks innumerable actions. So what does *God*-liness look like? It is living with God in the center of the picture. It is living with Him in focus wherever I go and whatever I do. Godliness is giving God His rightful place, His rightful awe, His worth and honor. But godliness is not some isolated set of religious activities. It is a mind-set that is focused on Him and an aroma that permeates our environment when we consciously carry Him into every conversation.

In 2 Peter 1:3, we see that "His divine power has given us everything we need for life and godliness." It is essential to see these two words as a compound and not a sequence. Life and godliness together are the two words

Peter chooses to summarize "everything." These are not two separate categories, as if there is the real life of work and money and family, but then there is another category called godliness. We know this because of the word Peter chose. *Bios* is one word for life, but it signifies life on the biological, physical level. This is the life of physical necessities like air, water, food, and shelter. But this is not the word Peter uses. Instead, his word is *zoe*, which depicts a quality of existence. *Zoe* is the word for vitality. *Zoe* animates the soul of the truly alive person. So when this is coupled with godliness, the impact of godliness is expanded to permeate all the facets of the truly alive person.

Godliness expands our spiritual borders. It is not meant to survive on the reservation of a few religious acres of our material lives, or in some spare, fidgety moments of a religious gathering each week. Godliness is designed to energize and vitalize every frontier of life.

But many of us have an approach-avoidance response to godliness. We have probably all practiced and recognized in others a fake form of godliness. In fact, counterfeit godliness is on clear display throughout the Bible. Cain claimed to be God-centered and concerned for God's honor, but he became angry with God when God did not look with favor on his offering. The Father saw through to his heart. The "sacrifice" was more about a performance Cain thought would placate God than a humble and costly expression of worship. Israel as a nation (see Isa. 1 and 2) staged impressive services of sacrifice, incense, and fasting. If godliness was next to gaudiness, they had it. But God rebukes them because this parade is all talk and no walk. They honored with their lips but held aloof their hearts. Jesus exposes the imitation godliness of the Pharisees.

Their prayers were profound, their giving was prodigious, and their rectitude was impervious to critique. But they were proud of their spiritual gymnastics and dithered on trivia while missing the weightier matters of justice, mercy, and love. In the early church, Ananias and Sapphira made a voluntary and noble pledge to endow the fledgling church. But their hearts were not in it. They skimmed their take off the top, tried to deceive the leadership, and offered the leftovers to God. It is recorded that they lied to the Holy Spirit, the exact opposite of true godliness.

Godliness gets misdirected when it is twisted it into an outward performance only—even a good and sacrificial activism. Instead of God as the goal and the motive, we can make it about the grade on our religious report card. It can so quickly be twisted into no longer being about the joy and adventure of learning and growing but about filling in all the blanks with the right answers. So Peter is not picturing godliness as a level we attain in the competition for God's affections and the world's admiration. Instead, it is a stance, a walk, an attitude that practices a consciousness of God's presence in all that we do and say. It's a humble, renewable practice, not an elite perch we attain. It's not something we get good at and then move on to other virtues. In fact, godliness always starts with that stark and exposing reflection in the mirror. It recurringly confronts us with our pale, disproportionate, and dodgy self. And we never get comfortable with what we see because it is our daily choice to be confronted, and compared, with true holiness. No one looks perfect in that mirror.

So will an uncompromising perspective on godliness lead us to paralyzed self-loathing? Will this stark and naked appraisal send us cowering from the challenges that await us? Will true godliness pummel me into imploded self-deprecation or send me fleeing into the desert? Not if Peter has anything to say about it! Godliness from Peter's perspective is essential equipment for "everything" we face in real life. It is essential to that effective and productive aliveness that is precious.

Practicing Repentance:

Just as staring in the mirror startles me into unavoidable and accurate self-assessment of my physical attributes, so the practice of godliness begins with stark truth about my spiritual condition. Godliness is not approached through more exercise but through humble self-examination, conviction, and repentance. Godliness is the recognition that all my disciplines, and all my intentionality and energy will never be enough. I will never stand comfortably alone, totally filled out and complete due to my own efforts. If I am to be a faithful and effective climber, I must become a practiced and disciplined repenter.

So how can this be good news? If godliness starts with recurring repentance, how will I ever advance beyond the quicksand of my own shame and weakness? Perhaps this aversive reaction is caused by a misunderstanding of the nature and the implications of repentance. Repentance is a doorway to renewed joy, not a pathway to incurable shame.

The word for repentance is *metanoia*, meaning a change of mind. John the Baptist came preaching in the desert, and his first word was "Repent!" Jesus called on the nation to repent. Paul and the other New Testament writers consistently call for repentance. But none of these teachers stopped where we seem to stop. True repentance always comes with a promise. The heaviness of sorrow brings the fresh air of restoration. "Repent, then, and turn to God, so that your sins may be wiped out, that times of refreshing may come from the Lord" (Acts 3:19).

See what this unflattering look into the mirror of holiness is meant to bring! Nothing but accurate reflections of our own sin, failure, incompleteness, and self-centeredness. But that's just the point! Repentance is the change of mind, the turning away from illusions and pride, and the turning toward the truth of the Father who loves and calls us to depend only on Him. Repentance is being arrested as we are speeding in the wrong direction and then turning around to come back home. And without this turning, this recurrent course correction, and restoration, the climb is just one long slog toward spiritual exhaustion.

Repentance has gained a bad reputation. Because of experiences of unforgiveness in our families of origin, or manipulations of our guilt, repentance has too frequently been associated with fear and shame, but not with refreshing! Repentance has led to an aftertaste of perpetual inadequacy and enslavement to an unpayable debt. And, dread of the next time it is necessary. But Paul points out that "Godly sorrow [caused by that look at imperfections in the mirror of holiness] brings repentance that leads to salvation *and leaves no regret"* (2 Corinthians 7:10; emphasis added). Repentance is the gateway to freedom. It begins in sorrow but results in joy! So, if repentance is meant to bring refreshing why am I not running toward it, realigning myself daily with God's own forgiveness and renewal?

My daughter's little girl, like all children, is adorable but constantly in need of guidance and correction. One day in her three-year-old frustration and demandingness, she bit her mother. Shelly immediately addressed this hurtful behavior: "That hurt Mommy. It makes Mommy very sad that you would bite her. It's wrong to ever bite someone." At this, that child's lip started to quiver, tears began to flow, and she said, "I'm sorry, Mommy." She instinctively reached out to hug and find reassurance from her mother. What do you suppose was Shelly's response? She smothered her repentant toddler in words of forgiveness and encompassed her in hugs and kisses. Repentance led to the wiping away of the sin, the affront, the rebellion, and was the means to restore a full and trusting relationship.

Many of us have not experienced the full cycle of repentance in this way.

Repentance has become associated with a one-way street of regret and shame. The restorative cycle has been truncated. As a result, repentance has seemed inseparable from shame, with recurring reminders of how to make up for it. In this context, repentance has become associated with the disease, not the cure. It has become a form of punishment, not the means to freedom. We have memories of someone yelling at us, poking an accusatory finger into our chest, and demanding that we say "Sorry." We have been leveraged into "repentance," which requires taking on an attribute of sorriness and defectiveness.

So who would ever want to look into the mirror of God's own holiness if this is the result of repentance? The answer would be "Never!" But two basic truths about repentance will draw us to be active practitioners of repentance and therefore pursuers of godliness:

1. Repentance is a means, not a goal. Repentance is looking into the mirror of God's unrefracted holiness and recognizing that my illusions about my own righteousness can only be sustained in the dark and through ignorance. I need all that Jesus Christ

has provided through His atoning death for me. The cross and Christ's atoning work on my behalf is my only hope of being counted righteous in God's eyes. Repentance is a means to get realigned in utter amazement and awe of God's compassion through the Gospel. I need this gospel today and every day! Repentance is practicing the Gospel, actually believing what I say I believe about grace. Repentance spurs me to preach the Gospel to myself again, and again, and again.

2. Repentance is a practice. Too often repentance is portrayed as that Damascus Road experience, that 180-degree turnaround from darkness to light. And, of course, it is just that at the moment of salvation. Repentance does involve deep conviction, raw emotion, and radical lifestyle change. But it is not to be reserved for those few special and spectacular interventions of conversion or revival. Though repentance should never become rote and routine, nevertheless it should become familiar. It should become a regular, daily, frequent means of reorientation to God's character, to godliness. It is spiritual hygiene, like brushing our teeth, which recognizes that fighting fleshly bacteria and spiritual plaque is best done daily.

Here is my definition of *repentance*:

Repentance is a fundamental reversal in my attitude toward a holy God, beginning with a deep conviction and fear of my own sin and its consequences. It is a deliberate turning from my own way and a turning to the Lord's way.

Repentance begins with confessing my sin and results in forgiveness, restoration, and childlike joy.

The godly are very familiar with repenting. A true disciple is a constant and practiced repenter. Godliness looks without pretense into the mirror of God's perfect nature and character. It's like looking at the wedding album and remembering the promises made. Godliness looks at what ought to be, and what actually is. Godliness asks humbly in every circumstance: "What part have I played in this tension, this misunderstanding, this isolation, this wounding?"

The apostle Paul writes to his protégé Timothy about his spiritual journey and sounds just like Peter. "Train yourself to be godly. For physical training is of some value, but godliness has value for all things, holding promise for both the present life and the life to come" (1 Tim. 4:7b–8). Godliness develops through training. Paul uses the word for "gymnasium" when he talks about training. He repeatedly uses physical training as a noble pursuit and a metaphor for spiritual development. However, he does put limits on the physical body, the physical world, and our present life. It has "some value." But this life and its goals, concerns, highs, and lows have limits.

Godliness, on the other hand, has an overarching benefit for both this life and the life to come. It has the advantage of being both temporally transforming and eternally rewarding. But it is not a competitive sport in which we judge winners and losers. How do we "add" godliness without keeping score?

It's all about the sequence. What comes first, and what comes second? Ephesians 5:1–2 makes it absolutely clear what comes first and what follows: "Be imitators of God, therefore, as dearly loved children and live a life of love, just as Christ loved us and gave Himself up for us as a fragrant offering and sacrifice to God."

If you are like me, your eyes are drawn to the action steps: "be imitators of God...live a life of love." These are dauntingly high standards, but they are not intended to be our focus. Notice the dependent clauses: "as dearly loved children...just as Christ loved us." This is where godliness is focused. This is the cause, the place to start every day. Start full!

Repentance does not lead us to performance to again try to prove our worthiness. No! It leads to forgiveness, cleansing, and freedom. We are brought back to the fullness, the richness, of God's grace in Christ. The brokenness of seeing myself in the mirror brings me helplessly but worshipfully back to the only source of good news for sinners. I am a dearly love child! Unaccountably, and completely contrary to every human transaction based on worth and performance, I start full when I again realize that I am loved with a love I could not earn and therefore can never lose. I start full every day, my lungs filled with the oxygen of pure grace. It is then, and only then, that I have His fullness and power to be an imitator of His character in my daily life.

Starting full every day is what produces radical change in the life of a disciple. As with a top-rope belay, when I know I can't fall, I tackle the hardest challenges with great confidence. Godliness on the inside produces godliness on the outside. But always in this order.

Look what happened when Zacchaeus was stunned by the grace of Jesus on the inside. Luke 19 records that this mercenary, money-driven tax collector who preyed on the weak and helpless was transformed. His eye-popping response to the forgiveness and grace of his new "Lord" was to give away half his possessions to the poor and vow to repay four times the amount he had defrauded. The sequence of this is unmistakable. Zacchaeus saw himself clearly, he repented, and then he responded freely with joyful obedience.

This kind of living shows the world what living Christianity looks like. It also reminds Jesus' followers that the path to effectiveness always passes through godliness.

For personal application:

1. How were you taught as a child to repent? Was the result healthy or unhealthy?

2. Think it through: why does genuine repentance lead to freedom and joy?

3. What are some disciplines that help you look into the mirror of God's holiness and see your true condition?

4. Why does godliness so easily get misdirected toward appearances and performance?

5. What crisis has made godliness a strong handhold that both humbled and sustained you?

---

[1] Don Mellor, *Rock Climbing*, (New York, NY, W. W. Norton and Company, 2003) p. 36

8

Safe Shelter

And to godliness, brotherly kindness…

—2 Peter 1:7

Handhold #7: Brotherly Kindness

Her tears glistened, then pooled, and finally ran freely down Marta's face. She sniffled her way through a wrenchingly painful story about her husband's losing battle with alcohol and the loss of a dream. The collateral damage from his addiction had forced her to be the breadwinner, the head of the household, and the sole nurturer of their two small children. Life was a combination of long days and tenuous nights. His absences became more protracted, and his brooding presence made things even worse. Marta found herself living on high alert whenever he was around. Volcanic anger had forced her many times to leave the house for long walks with the kids, hoping that he would cool down. Finally, for both safety and sanity, she filed for divorce.

Our acquaintance with Marta and Jacob began when my wife befriended Marta during a spring visit to a nearby greenhouse. Joanne noticed an accent in her English and asked what country she was from. Marta answered that she was in the US from Slovakia studying botany at the university. That conversation led to a supper on the patio with Marta and Jacob. The women were a match, and Jacob and I hit it off talking about cars and home remodeling.

Over the next several years, we dropped in occasionally, celebrated the birth of their first child, and walked through a time of grief when Jacob lost his father to lung cancer. It was during those days that we saw the deepening of Marta's faith and a spark in Jacob's spiritual interest. And then we learned that they planned to return to Slovakia. We were disappointed to see them go, but we understood their motivation to be near family. Another baby was born. Jacob looked hard for meaningful employment. They moved a couple of times. Alcohol began to drain his energy, his mood, and their marriage.

It had been a couple of years since the divorce, and now Marta was sitting at our table again. She had returned to see friends, and we longed to catch up on her life. After viewing pictures of the kids and talking about her work life, I dared to ask her the elephant-in-the-room question: "What happened between you and Jacob?" The story came slowly, first measured and careful, then eloquent and tearful. We anguished with a now single mom in her early thirties facing the prospect of raising her children without a daddy in the house. "What will you do now?" we asked.

The answer bore the sweet aroma of grace: the grace of God she was experiencing and the grace she was giving. She now lives with her mom, who provides childcare. Jacob has been afforded regular times with his children. He comes occasionally for a meal. She still loves him and wants the best for him. The children need to know and honor their dad, Marta said. She makes it a practice to speak well of their father and recognizes that he has an important role in their lives.

The remarkable work of grace in Marta's life is evident. The deep disappointments and betrayals that led to divorce have not metastasized into bitterness of spirit. In a word, Marta is kind to Jacob. She doesn't trust him totally, but she is kind. She has been repeatedly deceived by Jacob, but she is kind. She has had to bury many dreams because of Jacob's choices, but she is kind. She has chosen the next right thing in a difficult situation.

My friend Dave, who has a ministry of marriage counseling, shared a memorable phrase with me: "Compatibility is a given, but kindness is a choice." When couples come to him in the throes of conflict and bitterness, they often question whether they are, or ever were, compatible with each other. Dave explains that there have always been multiple connection points of compatibility, or they wouldn't have gotten married in the first place. The disconnect they are now experiencing comes not from a lack of compatibility but simply from a lack of choosing to be kind to each other. Sharp edges have come to characterize their interactions. Words, assumptions, daily inconveniences, and missed signals are handled with barbs of criticism and hand grenades of anger. Married couples sometimes treat each other without the least modicum of the civility that they would extend toward an anonymous clerk at Kwik Trip. Kindness, or lack of it, outs the inner spirit and sets the tone for all subsequent interaction.

And so we reach for the next handhold in the upward climb toward maturity. Coach Peter says, "Make every effort to add to your faith goodness, and to goodness, knowledge, and to knowledge, self-control; and to self-control, perseverance; and to perseverance, godliness; and to godliness, *brotherly kindness*, and to brotherly kindness, love" (2 Pet. 1:7; emphasis added).

The word is *philadelphia*. Brotherly love. It sounds pleasant and easy, but it is anything but that. The word implies more than mere willful tolerance or a benign lack of animosity. This is a blue-collar, hardworking, boots-on-the-ground choice. It invokes muscular concern, practical compassion, and tenacious generosity. This is the internal intention of the heart made visible and audible.

Brotherly kindness is a "best practices" kind of love. It is the kind of fellowship that shows itself receptive, resilient, and self-giving in the hard places. This is the doctrine of grace walking into inconvenience and serving up a warm meal. This is theoretical love of humanity put into practice with an irritable neighbor. Brotherly kindness takes a lofty vision statement and applies it at ground level to a recalcitrant crank. This is warm hospitality lavished on a sullen ingrate. Brotherly kindness stretches itself beyond forbearance to grasp the humanity behind the behavior and love the person on purpose.

Muscular love:

D. A. Carson[1] perceptively points out the real challenges to brotherly kindness within the body of Christ. Though we are exhorted to love the world and all the people in it, the real difficulty lies in practicing kindness and feeling affection for so many who live closest to us.

> "I suspect that one of the reasons why there are so many exhortations in the New Testament for Christians to love other Christians is because this is *not an easy thing to do...* The church is not made up of natural "friends." It is made up of natural enemies. What binds us together is not common education, common race, common income levels, common politics, common nationality, common accents, common jobs, or anything else of that sort. Christians come together, not because they form a natural collocation, but because they have all been

saved by Jesus Christ and owe him a common allegiance. In this light they are a band of natural enemies who love one another for Jesus' sake."[2]

Brotherly love does not expect the neighbor to change before he is loved. He is to be loved as he is found. What brotherly love brings to the world, to the neighbor, and to the body of Christ is an open face followed by open arms. It is love for my natural enemies, both big and small. It is an unconditional, positive regard for the actual persons hidden behind the layers of human foibles and societal distinctions.

My dad had a phrase: "Love chooses to understand." This was his approach to life, to difficult people, and his legacy for the home of my boyhood. I heard the phrase frequently at the dinner table as a child when a sister or two became insufferable. As a teenager, I grew weary of the phrase as the one bromide used to settle all critique, irritability, or injustice. It sounded too much like denial. But as my adult mileage has accumulated and the collection of challenging and strange characters has expanded, I have come to appreciate its deep wisdom. I can always choose to cling to the solid handhold of kindness. Words, actions, and motives are chosen. I am called to muscle up the will to understand. This is more than offering the benefit of the doubt. It is proactively giving the grace of expensive kindness.

There is a special note of urgency for the recipients of this letter from Coach Peter. Recall that Peter has addressed both of his letters to the body of Christ he describes as "strangers in the world, scattered throughout Pontus, Galatia, Cappadocia, Asia and Bithynia" (1 Pet. 1:1). This was not some quaint country church meeting in the white chapel pictured in a Vermont fall calendar. They are ethnically and culturally homeless. They were living as exiles, separated from their homeland, and "scattered" around the regions of modern-day northern Turkey and the Black Sea. Peter's letter didn't have a PO Box. It was hand-carried by Silas (1 Pet. 5:12) to these undocumented clusters of Christ followers.

Peter goes on to describe these believers as "aliens" (1 Pet. 2:11). If *strangers* denotes their cultural displacement, the word *alien* points to their legal status and personal identity. They had no rights, wealth, security, or claim in the society in which they lived. They were vulnerable to the politics and the power structures. While as believers they are climbing toward spiritual maturity, they are doing so as wanderers on earth, pilgrims, and refugees. They were disadvantaged in every way, and oppressed.

On top of that, these fledgling congregations were racially diverse. Some of them were Jews, and some were Gentiles. Nothing about their political or ethnic status was as volatile as this one fact.

The Jew-Gentile divide of Peter's day stretched back longer than a millennium. Within the living memory of each of these "aliens and strangers" whom Peter addresses is the repeated injustice suffered at the hands of the "other." Nothing in modern American racial tensions could match the age-old animosities between Jew and Gentile. A Jew prayed in thanks every day that he was not born a Gentile or a dog. Gentiles despised the cultic, separatistic, and aloof Jews. There was nothing either could find to love about the other. Wrongs and slights and brutalities between the groups were normal. But now the unthinkable has happened. Simultaneous with the revelation of the amazing grace of Jesus Christ that saved each one, individually, Jesus has made them "one new man out of the two, thus making peace" (Eph. 2:15). Jew and Gentile are now brought together into a new family. "And in this one body to reconcile both of them to God through the cross, by which he put to death their hostility" (Eph. 2:16).

As I write this, there are nationwide demonstrations sparked by the actions of white police officers in Ferguson, Missouri, and in New York City. The deaths of two African American men put a match to the dry tinder of old animosities between the races. Some are saying that this is only the latest chapter of racism that has gone unresolved in the United States for more than two hundred years. Each new incident reopens old wounds and stirs the coals of unrequited justice. Communities that seemed on the surface to be tolerating racial diversity have become enflamed overnight with old, layered, historic mistrust.

So what we are seeing here in this word *philadelphia* is not a call to mere civility so that everybody gets an equal share at the potluck. *Philadelphia* is the trumpet signal to march against the flow of history, race, and systemic hatreds. This brotherly kindness is a call for a radically new way of relating based on a fundamental redefinition of their identity. They are misfits in their culture. They are a congregation of natural enemies. They bear the scars of past wounds and ongoing suspicions fueled by society's norms. And all they have is each other. Peter writes, "Once you were not a people, but now you are the people of God…" (1 Pet. 2:10). The coach reminds his team: you are "a people belonging to God" (1 Pet. 2:9). Your marginalization in society does not define you. Your alien wandering does not define you. God's mercy through Jesus Christ is making of you a new nation, a new people, the living church, in which there is no Jew or Gentile (Gal. 3:28).

Brotherly kindness is to be the atmosphere you cultivate and share. In this way, the expanding, global, and interracial church becomes a new, welcoming community unique in the entire world. It's the new home for the dispossessed, with a new and immodest assignment: "To declare the praises of him who called you out of darkness into his wonderful light" (1 Pet. 2:9).

This proactive kindness that Peter admonishes surmounts huge hurdles like racism and classism. But it also climbs over the clutter of lesser, but irritating, habits and failings of fellow travelers. There are some people you can sit next to in a meeting, but you would hesitate to spend a vacation with them. Some people are certainly orthodox and theologically trustworthy, but they're hard to live with. Brotherly kindness is applied, not only to the stabs of outright prejudice but also to the paper cuts of irritation.

Brotherly kindness must thrive right inside every congregation of known, odd people. *Philadelphia* is the handhold to model maturity at the dinner table when family assumptions and demands clash. It is to be heard on the phone when the technical support associate doesn't understand our urgency. Kindness is to characterize the awkward drop-offs between divorced, custodial parents. Brotherly love is to be tenaciously gripped when a decision is made that affects my convenience. "As far as it depends on you," says Paul, "live peaceably with all" (Rom. 12:18).

A renewable resource:

Of course, this expensive gift of kindness would quickly be exhausted if I had to generate this sweetness myself. It must be consistently renewed. It is of a different origin and species than mere niceness or moralistic civility. *Philadelphia* originates in my own experience of God's lavish grace in Jesus Christ. This rescue, this mercy, and this unmerited love are the Gospel that birthed us. And this Gospel is a daily supply of grace upon grace. Only because the Christ-one has experienced this grace can he or she afford to grant it to others.

Kindness is the Spirit's produce. Rooted in grace, kindness flourishes as the visible fruit. It is both proactive and preventive. We are to "put on kindness" (Col. 3:12) in order to pursue unity in the body of Christ. And we are to practice kindness under pressure in the wider culture so there are no obstacles in the way of our Gospel witness (2 Cor. 6:3–6). Either way, it is the fruit of the Holy Spirit working in his people (Gal. 5:22), not only to preserve us from disintegration but also to propel us into tireless engagement with a prickly culture.

This exploration of our next handhold may evoke a nod of recognition, a pang of conviction, or even a renewed resolve to stretch upward toward higher ground. We can all think of countless opportunities to show more brotherly kindness to the scruffy saints inside the church, the surly commuters outside its walls, and the spouse with whom we share toothpaste.

But altruistic intentions, and frequent resolutions, seem to stumble over some unseen trip wires. We are preconditioned and weakened by our culture and media more deeply than we recognize. Fed by talking points, party politics, opinion pieces, and talk radio hyperbole, our appetites crave anything but brotherly kindness. We can become addicted to being mad, adrenalized by offense, and tantalized by gossip. We are accustomed to not hearing one kind thing said about the "other." We tend to watch

the programs that nurture our own cherished biases. It
will take great grace, coupled with willful tenacity, to move
against the tide of tearing down, and toward the goal of
building up.

Clearing the landmines:

Landmines to brotherly kindness are planted everywhere
we walk. Recognizing them, and disarming them, will
engender opportunities to freely march into God's
purposes. These landmines are embedded in the soil of our
thinking. Not only do we not think Christianly, we often
fail to even think logically. Exposing a few of them is the
essential work of maturity. Disarming them will give new
life to *philadelphia*.

Landmine 1: Sloganeering. This is the fallacy of jumping
to a conclusion before you have sufficient data. When a
general conclusion is drawn on a sample or database that
is too small, it is logically erroneous. It's lazy thinking that
lolls away on canned clichés and editorialist's opinions
rather than doing the rigorous work of listening, learning,
and discerning.

One predictable by-product of sloganeering is
stereotyping. This is not only ungracious as an outcome,
but it is illogical at its roots. The result is wrong morally, but
it starts with being wrong intellectually. A believer's mind
is being renewed (Rom. 12:2) not only to see things from a
spiritual perspective he has never before contemplated but
also to cast out foolishness and every form of logical fallacy.

Kindness plummets when I rely on faulty, hasty
generalizations. If my mind allows twelve-second sound
bites to define complex issues, a person or a group, I won't
see the humanity that deserves kindness. And so kindness

is stillborn because of slogans, talking points, and hasty conclusions that preclude its viability.

Landmine 2: Black or white thinking. This error in thinking occurs when we suppose that in any given situation, there are only two alternatives. The decision is binary. It's an on-off switch. Either-or. It's you or me. Win or lose.

As a pastor, I have seen this frequently. A passionate, and energetic activist has a cause. He comes to me with a clarity that is unassailable. Something must be done! The moral and spiritual crisis is real and at the door. "Pastor, we must mobilize everyone to face this down." This is the hour, and God's people are the answer.

The problem has come when, even if I did support the effort, and the church responded with energy, it wasn't enough. For him, this is the only issue on the planet. The battle lines are drawn. He believes it is the last stand for truth. Unless it becomes the only issue for me, and for the entire church, we are not serious. The slammed-door departure from the church of such prophets has usually been accompanied by words and letters that were anything but kind. My character and integrity of our ministry were assessed with scathing accusation and dire predictions. The demandingness of such a crusader is revealed by their all-or-nothing rigidity, and damage is done. But it is the faulty, illogical thought pattern that drove such unkind reactions.

Our culture encourages black-or-white thinking. It's engrained in our political talking points and our coffee-break councils. Nuance is too complex. Context takes too long to understand. And when the mind is preset with this kind of thinking it becomes like a mousetrap that is either benign or deadly, depending on where you step. Kindness toward a laggardly coworker, a former spouse, a political challenger, or a person from a different culture will not survive in a mousetrap worldview.

Brotherly kindness finds a way to maintain moral integrity while entering into the mess. Good intentions toward kindness may be spiritually passionate, but they will not survive a thought pattern that requires an easy solution. Kindness does not guarantee that the recipient's life will miraculously change. Kindness is given to the person who sometimes bites the hand that feeds him, rejects the obvious solution, snarls at the gift offered, and swallows generosity in a black hole of neediness.

If the scarred lives surrounding us are painted only in black and white, kindness will have every excuse to stay in its bunker of self-righteous apathy. But if kindness is meant for the real world, we will press into the headwinds of the mess, recognizing that complexity is the native habitat of spiritual maturity.

One summer, a young man appeared in our youth group out of nowhere. His résumé was immediately impressive. He touted that he had been recruited by the University of Colorado as a quarterback. The other students were in awe. He was musical, funny, and spoke of exploits that sounded too good to be true. They were. None of it was true. So, after Ray had burned through every relationship in his family and our church, he found himself literally homeless. No one trusted him. I convinced him to go with me to the Denver Rescue Mission for temporary food and shelter.

The mission was administered by Leroy ("Brad") Bradrick, a long-time friend of our family. He was a no-nonsense former pastor who was street savvy but tireless in generosity toward men with chronic personal problems.

He ran a tight ship, but it was safe, clean, and on mission for Jesus. Ray was much younger than the usual population, but Brad said he could stay as long as he could abide by the rules. That lasted about forty-eight hours. Ray bolted, but not before stealing some equipment from the mission and leaving a trail of volatile confrontations with other guests.

I drove to the mission to apologize to Brad for the disruption and stress that Ray had caused. "I'm sorry, Brad," I said. "You opened your doors to Ray, and he turned around and kicked you in the face." I will never forget the reply of this veteran caregiver. Without skipping a beat, Brad replied, "Don't worry about it. We're pretty tough in the face around here." That was pure kindness toward me, but also toward the most recent vandal of the shalom of the Denver Rescue Mission. Kindness was not killed by the messiness of a real hard-to-love person.

Landmine 3: Motive assignment. It's an oh-so-easy slip to make. An action or a word strikes me as untrue, unfair, or wrongheaded. Before I know it, I'm assessing the motive and character of the person. The words said or the policies pursued cannot possibly have merit because of the obvious, selfish motive I have presumed lies behind them.

Sometimes we call this by a clearer, harsher name: character assassination. If the motive and character of the actor or speaker are "known" to be evil, then any word or policy coming from them is obviously tainted. Thus, I am free to dismiss the ideas as scurrilous, or at least irrelevant. Nothing good could ever come from him or her. I can therefore distance myself from this person. The brotherly kindness to engage in dialogue, to seek to truly understand their viewpoint, and to treat another with humble respect will never gain a foothold if the mind is already repulsed by a purported dark motive.

There are many forms of "motive assignment" in the Christian community. A few years ago during the burgeoning spiritual formation movement, some brothers and sisters in our fellowship became quite concerned that an author who wrote on the subject of Christian meditation had employed techniques borrowed from Eastern mysticism. The fact that he had written helpfully for decades on numerous other subjects was suddenly irrelevant. Because this one aspect of his writing was disagreeable and appeared dangerous to some, the entire catalog of his work was dismissed as heretical by these brethren. Further, I became suspect when I quoted him on an entirely different subject, about which there was clear biblical support. Since his heart motive had already been assessed by his critics, nothing he said on any subject could be trusted. Instead of simply disagreeing when an author lacked discernment, they cut themselves off from a treasure trove of biblical insight that had flowed from his life for decades.

As the evangelical church engages the culture over a number of hot-button issues, from abortion, to same-sex marriage, to war, and the First Amendment, we are not aided by the thought pattern which assigns motive first and asks questions later. Both inside and outside the church, kindness will only be possible if we learn to exercise the mental discipline to engage the argument on its merits, and not slur the messenger with innuendo and purported evil motives.

Brotherly kindness is one of the life-sustaining handholds we must master in order to be effective and productive in our spiritual lives. Here are some exercises to strengthen this grip. These eight habits will fortify your practice of brotherly kindness in an increasingly adverse and harsh environment.

Eight Habits of Kindness

1. Listen: ask questions for clarity. You will know you have listened when you can state the person's idea or proposal back to them in your own words with their assent.

2. Original sources: refuse to perpetuate opinion. Seek out the source in context before reacting or spinning the editorialized or sensationalized rumor.

3. Silence: if you don't know, don't speak.

4. Defend: give the benefit of the doubt. When a friend brings a grievance based on an action or word of another, a general defense of that person's character can pave the road toward kindness. A kindness-sowing response might be, "That seems out of character for the person I know him to be. Have you talked to him about it, or can I go with you to gain clarity?"

5. Exercise the "vague but true" principle: When there is an unresolved conflict between yourself and another person, or a rift within the group or community, don't proliferate stumbling blocks by spreading specifics. Pave the way toward kindness by being purposely short on details but truthful about the issue. "Yes, we currently have not arrived at agreement, but you can pray for us in the process." That's truthful but vague. It tamps down the innate desire

for onlookers to know the "dirt" on the other person. But too much detail gives unwarranted access into confidential matters and often provides ammunition for dis-unifying rumors.

6. Study Ephesians 4:29–31

7. Memorize Philippians 4:8–9

8. Move: Brotherly kindness does not just roll into place. It must be lifted from inertia and placed in motion. It's my move. What can I do in thought, action, or word to replace the tang of bitterness with the savor of kindness—first in myself and then toward the other.

Before we leave this subject, we are reminded that Peter does not just jump into a list of moralisms and behavior codes to make the church straighten up. He starts from the deepest well of salvation where we all receive "grace and peace" through Jesus Christ. Only from this refreshing and artesian source can fresh kindness bubble up into our parched world.

Random acts of kindness are beautiful, but purposeful acts of kindness leave an aroma of grace. I coaxed from Daryl his story of giving kindness. He had been the manager of a small grocery store in a northern suburb of Minneapolis before moving to our neighborhood, some twenty-five miles to the south. During his tenure as manager he had helped an elderly woman with her shopping. She came at the same time every week. He personally made sure her groceries were bagged and loaded in her car. When she could no longer drive, he picked her up after work hours, allowed her the dignity of doing her own shopping, returned her to her residence, and put away her groceries.

The sweet aroma of Daryl's kindness reaches a heartwarming crescendo. When he moved to our suburb, he continued this lavish kindness! Every week he drove north to fulfill a mission known only to him and one other person. He continued until the day this widow passed away. When I heard of this unseen, eloquent testimony of kindness I knew that the grace of Jesus in Daryl's life was the only explanation for such grace to be shown to another. And the aroma still lingers.

As a testimony to the world, kindness is the next right thing. It will shine as an incandescent brightness against the dark rules of the jungle that savage human hope. As the DNA of a living church, brotherly kindness is the next right thing for guarding, and enhancing every relationship. Doses of kindness given and received every day will remind us of the redemption which transforms us from the biting and devouring which came naturally to us before grace taught us a new way.

For personal application:

1. Why is it sometimes easier to show kindness to a stranger than to someone we know well?

2. Who is one disagreeable person in your workplace to whom you could show kindness?

3. Does being kind require that we deny real problems or bury our own needs?

4. What might be a risky form of brotherly kindness because your actions might be misinterpreted by the culture or your church?

5. When should you cling to this handhold because it is the next right thing to do?

---

[1] D. A. Carson, *Love in Hard Places*, (Wheaton, Ill, Crossway Books, 2002) p 61

[2] ibid

9

$$\infty$$

Summiting

Add love…

Handhold #8: Love

 The Vendée Globe is the most extreme long-distance sailing race in the world. The rules are simple. The winner is the first sailor to cross the finish line after having circumnavigated the globe, single-handedly, without stopping. Twenty-seven thousand miles are navigated utterly alone, but the heart of darkness is the Southern Ocean. Six to eight weeks of prodigious effort and courage is required to get through it. It's a realm where sheer survival is at stake every moment. Mountainous seas five stories tall, brutal winds, and complete isolation combine to challenge the pluck of the saltiest of sailors. Only a few astronauts have ever been farther from land than these boats in the vast remoteness of the Southern Ocean.

Christmas day 1997 brought disaster to one of the ten boats still in the race. Raphael Dinelli's boat capsized in fifty-foot waves and seventy-mile-per-hour winds. He lashed himself to the upturned hull and sent a satellite-borne distress signal.

But who could possibly help? The longest range aircraft could barely fly the round-trip, much less offer any help even if they could spot him. His only hope to be rescued from hypothermic death was another sailor, a fellow competitor, Pete Goss.

Problem was, Goss was 160 miles downwind, surfing mountainous waves under bare masts, just trying to survive himself. But once notified by race officials that Dinelli was in distress, Goss put the race, his boat, and his very life at risk to attempt a rescue. Two days of beating back against the wind, his masts knocked horizontal every half hour, and his boat subjected to stresses never imagined by its builders brought him to the life raft where Dinelli was nearly comatose.

Dinelli and Goss were not best buddies. They had no relationship to speak of, except their common cause to beat each other to the finish line. One was English and the other French, opponents in an ocean-going chess match. But when the rescue of the helpless could be accomplished only by the greatest cost to the rescuer, something overrode their competitiveness and fused them together as brothers.

A great deal more than raw courage was displayed. Pete Goss abandoned his goals for which he had trained and sacrificed for years. He put his sponsor's investments at risk. He went without food or sleep, under battering conditions, and fought his own fears at the crest of every wave. Whether he knew it at the time or not, he demonstrated the best definition of love ever uttered: "Greater love has no one than this, that a man lays down his life for his friends" (John 15:13).

But this willful labor of love was soon to be transformed into an emotional feeling of love. Raphael and Pete began a friendship during that intense experience. "We're like brothers now. We'll be friends for the rest of our lives."[1] After Dinelli's recovery, he invited Pete Goss to stand as his best man at his wedding, and they also teamed up in a transatlantic race. Love that was first muscled up as a hard decision has been taken flight into mutual brotherhood.

When I began rock climbing in the High Sierras of California, I was motivated by sheer adventure, but especially by the thought of standing on the summit, the ultimate goal of all climbing. Most of the peaks we scaled were walk-ups and didn't demand a lot of technical skill nor much real risk. The hard work was just getting there: hiking and camping for several days just to get to the actual climb. That sweaty work didn't lack reward. There were quiet trails, lush meadows bedecked with wildflowers, azure-blue summer skies, and frigid alpine lakes. But this whole bundle of experiences was a prelude to one thing: summiting.

This wasn't just a nature hike with friends or the exploits of a few climbing buddies out for an adventure. I was climbing with troubled, incorrigible young men. I was a counselor for a camp, utilizing "stress camping" to build teamwork among wayward boys who were assigned to us through the California Youth Authority. They were serving sentences under medium security for a variety of delinquent activities. *Sea and Summit*, the ministry I served in those days of my own spiritual apprenticeship, received these young men straight out of the juvenile camps under orders from the courts. We took them for twenty-one days into an experience they would never forget.

Our strategy was to take them out of their element, away from their props. We wanted to teach and model what it was like to trust someone and to have someone trust you—on the end of a belay or rappel. We hoped to show them a level of joy and satisfaction that would never be gained through drugs, violence, and gang conformity. We placed them in "watches" of four members plus one counselor and had them eat, train, climb, wash dishes, and run together. Everybody participated, or the whole group received consequences. Ultimately we wanted to introduce them to the Man of all men, Jesus Christ. But first we wanted to speak into their lives from a stance of trustworthiness and hope, something most of them knew little about.

Our goal after a week of training, outfitting, and preparing these young men was to get the whole group to the top of the mountain together. Two or three hot and dusty days on the trail were spent getting to our base camp. Then on the day of our climb, we rose at daylight so that we could summit as early as possible to avoid afternoon thunderstorms and lightning. We also wanted to take time to celebrate by eating our meager backpack lunch at the summit, savoring a breathtaking 360-degree panorama.

I remember those summits like they were yesterday. There was worship there. It wasn't formalized with hymns and spoken prayers. This was the primordial worship that lies dormant in every heart and which is evoked by sheer majesty. City boys were pointing, gawking, staring, and basking. Beauty captivated. Grandeur silenced. Satisfaction from the hard-won victory settled deep in each soul. Every city kid had that one-hundred-mile gaze. There was a communion of understanding, a shared brotherhood of sweat and suffering. Those morsels of tuna fish, Triscuits, Fig Newtons, and dried apricots were savored like sacraments, washed down with a tin cup full of Kool-Aid. Then, finally, with the afternoon sun advancing across the sky and summoning us to leave this capsule of tranquility, we held our final ceremony. We solemnly signed our names to the climbing register.

At the summit of each peak is a six-inch length of galvanized pipe with screwed-on end caps. Rolled inside that pipe is a pencil and a few pages with a growing list of those who have summited the peak. Each of these boys, using their best penmanship, signed their name and date.

It was a sacred document, a certificate only understood and valued by the other signatories. And now these boys from the 'hoods of Los Angeles, Bakersfield, Oakland, and Riverside signed a certificate possibly more meaningful than a diploma from any school they had ever attended. It declared, "I was here! I was all here, every cell of me. I was here under the blazing sun, after a long hike in, and a long slog up. I was here to see what you saw, and we all shared. I was here, and I'll never forget standing on this very spot and knowing what the summit is all about."

Love Is All You Need

If there is any summit in human experience, it is love. It, too, may require a long trail and a hard climb in order to arrive, but it is worth every arduous step. And nothing compels us onward like the quest to give and experience love. If there is any shared goal, shared work, shared joy desired by the religious and irreligious alike, it is love. This is the summit to which our climbing coach has led us. The summit of love, once experienced, remains both an indelible memory and an insatiable quest for the rest of our lives.

A sense of total sensory, soulish, and physical well-being comes at those summits where love is understood in its depth and beauty. It is here that the panorama of life can be savored safely, freely, together, in the warming sun. It is at these summits that we leave lesser struggles behind and gain perspective on the long journey we have traveled. When we gaze at life from the summit, we not only see the arduous trail that now lies behind us, but we also envision challenges we want to explore out into the future.

Yet what more can be said about love that hasn't already been said or sung? Based on the Top 40 playlist, our appetite for replays of classic oldies, and the enduring big band favorite songs, one would think that our society lives and breathes love. Just look at some of the 3,500 songs that have *love* in their title:

- All You Need Is Love
- Love Will Keep Us Together
- I Will Always Love You
- I Just Called to Say I Love You
- Crazy Stupid Love
- The Power of Love
- Crazy in Love
- Where Is the Love?
- I Can't Stop Loving You
- Best of My Love

We croon about love, talk the politics of love, and fantasize and make movies about love. But based on the recurrence of violent crimes, wars, wounded hearts, petty grievances, celebrity breakups, and stagnant marriages, do we know anything about love, really? Given all the pining, crying, craving, and promising that gush through popular culture, one would think that love is our native language and habitat.

But in fact, *love* is perhaps the most shape-shifting word in our vocabulary. It can be used to mobilize the masses to eradicate injustice or help earthquake victims. Then in the next moment, it is used in a sound bite to justify someone's demanding narcissism or lack of self-control. Love is sold as the promised dividend when you sign up for that vacation cruise, shower with that bar of soap, or buy that new car. "Love. It's what makes a Subaru a Subaru."

Love is leveraged as the justification to pass new laws, to obliterate old moral boundaries, and shift public funding toward new entitlements. Love is variously portrayed as an amalgam of emotion, motive, and action. Love is touted as a goal, a means, a purpose or an ideal, depending on how we want to leverage it. It is shaped into whatever we want it to be. It's a universally held assumption in desperate need of a clear definition.

To add weight to this need for clarity, here's a unique and startling convergence: both the Bible and pop culture agree about the priority of love! Love is at the top of the charts and the pinnacle of all the virtues. Love is the answer to so many of the needs, longings, omissions, and commissions of a hurting world. John Lennon and the apostle John agree: love is all you need. The only question is, what is love?

Our climbing coach Peter has led us toward this summit. Even though I have tried to avoid viewing these handholds of spiritual progress as a ladder of accomplishment or ascending levels of sanctification, it is impossible not to see love as the summit of our spiritual quest. As Paul asserts in his great poem to love in 1 Corinthians 13, I can exercise every other noble-sounding and heroic quality, but if I am devoid of love, there is no progress in me and no effectiveness through me.

Love is at the top. It is both the goal and the means of every other virtue. And so Peter, in his understated way, reminds me that love is the aim. Love is the apex. Love is the peak experience.

Add "to brotherly kindness, love," (2 Pet. 1:7).

Getting Our Bearings

One of the beauties of Scripture is its self-consistency. When it comes to the centrality of love, we find a deep, resonant harmony stretching from the daily prayer of the righteous Israelite in the Shema (Deut. 6:5) to the teaching of Jesus in Luke 10:27, where He underscores the centrality of the commands to love: "Love the Lord your God with all your strength and with all your mind, and your neighbor as yourself." Likewise, we find the teaching of Peter and John in complete harmony with the teaching of Paul, even though they probably never saw one another after the earliest days of their apostleship. They ministered to different cultures and separate churches but arrived at the same summit. Paul captures in one sentence (Gal. 5:6; emphasis added) what Peter unpacks in his list of handholds: "The only thing that matters is *faith expressing itself through love*." 2 Peter 1:5–8 shows what love expressing itself looks like: add goodness, knowledge, self-control, perseverance, godliness, and brotherly kindness. So, Paul and Peter agree: faith starts the climb, the character of Christ in the believer advances the climb, and love is the summit!

Given this harmony of the Scriptures, we can confidently take our bearings from the best guidebook to this summit of love, found in 1 Corinthians 13. This is the most classic and compact ode to love ever written.

> *If I speak in the tongues of men or of angels, but do not have love, I am only a resounding gong or a clanging cymbal. If I have the gift of prophecy and can fathom all mysteries and all knowledge, and if I have a faith that can move mountains, but do not have love, I am nothing. If I give all I possess to the poor and give over*

my body to hardship that I may boast, but do not have love, I gain nothing.

Love is patient, love is kind. It does not envy, it does not boast, it is not proud. It does not dishonor others, it is not self-seeking, it is not easily angered, it keeps no record of wrongs. Love does not delight in evil but rejoices with the truth. It always protects, always trusts, always hopes, always perseveres.

Love never fails. But where there are prophecies, they will cease; where there are tongues, they will be stilled; where there is knowledge, it will pass away. For we know in part and we prophesy in part, but when completeness comes, what is in part disappears. When I was a child, I talked like a child, I thought like a child, I reasoned like a child. When I became a man, I put the ways of childhood behind me. For now we see only a reflection as in a mirror; then we shall see face to face. Now I know in part; then I shall know fully, even as I am fully known.

And now these three remain: faith, hope and love. But the greatest of these is love.

The first thing I learn about love is the hardest thing to swallow. It's not about me! It's not about developing my Hallmark card eloquence. Words alone, sung, written, or said, won't cut it if there is no substance behind them. Nor is it about the profundity of my wisdom or the spectacular usefulness of my spiritual gifts. Love will fail to launch; it will amount to nothing if theology doesn't become biography. Furthermore, impressive generosity, even to the point of martyrdom for a noble cause, will leave no lasting fruit unless the unseen motivation of love is its driving force.

So Paul strips away the three most prevalent pedigrees claimed by those of us who purport to love. Lofty, emotional words; deep and fervent spirituality; and sacrificial action do not prove that I have understood love. They each may be employed in the delivery of love but not until they become the servants of love itself.

Discovering what love really is, is not just a good idea. Love is what God is (1 John 4:8)! Love is the ultimate measure of my contribution in life. The final evaluator of my life is: did I find love and did I give love? During my journey on this earth, did I give the most essential thing? Did I generously pass on what I received from the Father? Did anyone's life receive the one investment from me that will last forever? Did I spend enough time at the summit luxuriating in the warmth and wonder of God's love? The "greatest" of all the things in life is love.

So this is where the challenge begins. And it isn't just a challenge to our culture, whose view of love has been shaped by Hollywood movies, Nashville music, and soap opera trysts. It's a challenge to all cultures and for all of humanity. Paul wades into the deep end of ancient world philosophies to challenge their view of love: the Stoics who denigrated pleasure and the Epicureans who embraced sensuality. Paul wrote to the Corinthian church, some of whom were slaves to pleasure and others who were proud of their asceticism. To all of them, he lays down a clear plumb line by which to assess the quality of their love. It's a timeless straightedge, accessible to anyone, no matter their eloquence, spiritual maturity, or circumstance. But first we must learn what love is.

Love Says *No*

There are two key words that collect all the nuances of love. *Patient* is the summation of love's many restraints where it says *no* to self-interest. *Kind* is the summary for love's selfless investments where it says *yes* to the needs of another.

Love says *no* to a host of impatient, reflexive emotions, bad habits, self-serving actions, and devious motives. Love is patient because it does not resort to the quick-fix reactions that have my immediate comfort and status as their goal. So love is never envious, boastful, proud, rude, self-seeking, easily angered, begrudging, or joyful with evil (1 Cor. 13:4–6). Love is patient, taking the long view, preserving relationships in spite of hurtful affronts and stinging paper cuts. It does not use power, language, or hidden agendas to feather its own nest. Love doesn't lose track of the goal.

My friend Ron recently set out to hike the Appalachian Trail. It had been his dream for many years to start in Georgia and end in Maine, two thousand miles later. However, he didn't plan to do it all at once. Starting in April, Ron learned about rain. He learned about obstreperous and strange fellow hikers. He learned about crowded shelters, bears, mosquitoes, and mud. But the most important takeaway from his first two weeks on the trail came at a hostel for hikers. There, sixty miles into the hike, was a guide who offered invaluable information. He showed each hiker the unneeded gear he was lugging in his pack. He isolated the extraneous from the essential so that the ultimate goal became more accessible. Ron unburdened himself of fifteen pounds of unnecessary stuff.

When love says no it is unburdening itself of a pile of extraneous gear that needs to be discarded. These weights will not help me accomplish the mission. Love, true love, says no to a pile of pride-generated amenities that are standard equipment for a strategy of self-protection. I may feel I need this kind of equipment for shelter when

I'm concerned for my comfort, my pleasure, or my ego gratification. But when I begin this quest for a life that makes a difference to others and leaves the sweet aroma of purpose and legacy, I recognize that the stuff of the past is a hindrance to a greater yes. So, I say no to the hot-tub me-ism, the face-saving cosmetics, and the touchy demandingness that is my inborn nature. They are all dead weight that will impede my progress toward the goal.

This disciplined discarding doesn't usually get generated from a classroom theory. We normally have to learn it on the trail, when our comforts and expectations crash into reality, when wear and fatigue teach us the consequences of our assumptions. It registers with us in the daily commute that takes us from selfishness to sacrifice. It's a part of the journey that must be walked in order to make any friendship, marriage, or a family function.

When I got married, my backpack of assumptions was loaded with self-interest. Then, I really learned how selfish I could be as I walked into the warm nest of parenthood. It wasn't until I began sharing my space, my time, my schedule, and my sleep with a baby that I came face-to-face with the unloving reflexes of my heart. It would be 2:00 a.m., and I would awaken to a cry. Every fiber in me said yes to selfishness. I would lie still, faking a deep REM sleep, hoping that my wife would drag herself out from under warm covers onto the cold floor and attend to our intrusive offspring. I was tired. I needed my sleep. This interruption could take five minutes or a couple hours. I can't afford to be tired today. I have important things to be alert for. Somebody else (wonder who that could be?) should sacrifice. Not me.

But love tenaciously coaches me to say no to that naturally selfish me. It says no to craven comforts and manipulations of others and rises to care for the child while granting sleep to my wife. Nice theory. Tough application.

When love says no, it isn't looking for applause. No cameras are rolling. Love saying no to self-interest is reality, not a reality show. In fact, most of what love does goes without notice. It never makes the headlines, and it doesn't waft along to a sound track. It simply says a silent but robust no to an endless list of selfish reflexes, reactions, and rationalizations we may have practiced and harbored for a lifetime.

When Paul says love is patient, he uses a word that is translated in older English as "longsuffering." This kind of longsuffering does not just give up, muttering "Whatever!" in exasperated resignation. Nor is it just sleep-walking compliance or the joyless drudgery of sheer self-denial. No, patience is a prime characteristic of love that is fed to us by the Spirit of Jesus who lives in us. It is a garment of Christlikeness meant to be put on, repeatedly. It is choosing to be teachable and coachable. When I love, it means I have a willingness to be shown what I look like in action. I look into the mirror of God's Word, and I watch the wake I'm leaving in the lives of others.

To love is to put away my childish ways—to set aside childish tactics. Growing up in love means recognizing that instant gratification is childish. Maturity resets my expectations about everyone else and installs a new vigilance. Love muscles up and trains itself to meet error and insult with daily endurance. This patience is not easily provoked because it is tenaciously goal oriented. The eye is on the prize, so love says no to diversions and shortcuts, most of which are designed to give me a break at a high cost to others.

As I write this, the Animas River in Colorado has been transformed from a pristine rafting and fishing mountain stream into a slurry the color of mustard. It's the result of a toxic spill of gold mining waste. Everyone downstream will feel the effects for years. Prevention would have been far better than any proposed cure.

And that is true for relationships as well. The Animas River debacle caused me to recall another toxic spill that happened just weeks before. It wasn't in the mountains; it was in my office. It wasn't poisonous chemicals, but toxic words. I met with a couple who said they were desperate for some help in their marriage. I began by getting some background. "What brings you here?" I asked. It was like breaching a toxic reservoir.

"We're here because we don't communicate," she said.

"Well, at least you don't," he replied. "You're too busy with your degree program, which we never agreed on, and your Facebook addiction and your secrets. Who can communicate to someone who isn't there?"

"See, Pastor, this is what always happens. He hasn't forgiven me for an affair I had two years ago, and everything I do now just brings rejection and abuse."

"Well, I can't trust her," he protested. "She's absent for the kids, she flirts at the office, and the house is a total disaster. I have to do everything, and I'm tired of being the only adult in the relationship."

"He hates my family."

"Your family is twisted and dysfunctional."

"You have never loved me or cherished me as your wife."

"I never should have married you in the first place."

And it only got worse from there. The crudeness of their shutdowns of each other, the name-calling, and the blaming was endless. I had to call a timeout, and all I could do was display the tears in my eyes that two Christians could speak to each other like this. They were so accustomed to the poisonous sludge of hurtful words that they didn't even notice the destruction anymore. They seemed emotionally numb to the brutality they were both dishing out, but I was dumbstruck and profoundly saddened.

They didn't really want counsel for their marriage or insight into their own contribution to this mess. They each wanted vindication and recognition that they were married to the most selfish person in the universe. Each was proud, rude, self-seeking, furiously angry, with a well-rehearsed record of heinous wrongs committed against them. And each refused to give it up or to restrain their most vicious recriminations. They could not conceive of saying no to their offended self-righteousness. And all I could think about was three teenagers who were living downstream from this poison.

When love says no to the self-centered venting of hateful words and no to stockpiled indictments to be unleashed in the future, it is doing something essential for the ecology of a relationship. It is preventing the pollution of marriages, of whole family systems, office cultures, small group community, and church unity. It is a preservation of the stream that gives life, and beauty, and enjoyment. When love says no, it is remembering that everything flows downstream, especially words. No matter how thorough the cleanup might eventually be, these words can never be completely recovered. A residue is left that will have incalculable consequence in multiple lives.

Paul aims a laser beam on what needs to stop if love is to flourish. "Put off your old self, which belongs to your former manner of life and is corrupt through deceitful desires" (Eph. 4:22). This patient love doesn't come naturally! It's not something I just fall into or master instantly by following my heart. It's the ultimate summit of life toward which I need to deliberately ascend by jettisoning a host of responses that seem natural to me. That old me is corrupt, deceitful, and deceived. Scripture counsels me to stop lugging this useless baggage so that I can ascend to the summit of love.

To love requires that I need to say no to the old and yes to the new. I need to learn patience by resisting the inbuilt reflex to turn to old bankrupt comforts. Love will refuse to sink into old disfiguring greed. Love restrains and will not lob those old verbal bombs. Love does not nurse old viral bitterness nor old cynical vengeance. Love will not sneak out the door to indulge in old selfish sensuality, fantasy, or pornography. In short, love consistently says a resounding no to that old me that was entirely self-seeking. This insistent no to the old self is the headwaters for a life-giving stream of genuine love that flows toward others.

Love Says *Yes*

To love is to do what you want. That last word is all-important. What do I really "want" from life? Who do I want to become? What do I want others to remember about me? Wanting is not to be confused with wishing or feeling. Wanting is the practiced, regular installment toward a desired outcome. And—be careful here—wanting is not the same as feeling. In fact, my wants should frequently trump how I feel. This is not just semantics.

Almost every year I have taken some kind of bicycle trip with a group of men. We typically ride about seventy-five miles per day for four days. It's an opportunity for friendship, camaraderie, and transparent sharing around the campfire. I want to go on these trips, but they are not easy. I want to be in good enough physical condition to enjoy the trip. But I don't always feel like putting in the miles of training. It is then that my feelings are overruled by what I truly want. So, I do what I want, not what I momentarily feel like doing. Loving is like that. Love is what I really want.

Paul extols love as proactive. It is kind. Love says yes to the hard work of consistently giving itself away because it wants the best outcome and the highest reward. Real love progresses from the internal purifying of motives toward the unstoppable investment in others. This is love's direction. This is love's work. This is what love wants. In biblical terms, it always "rejoices with the truth, protects, trusts, hopes and perseveres" (1 Cor. 13:7).

This may sound exhausting and superhuman, but not if I know what I want. If I want a mutually fulfilling, lifelong, ever-growing relationship with one intimate lover and friend, I will invest all the positive qualities of love into my marriage. If I want the fragrance of grace to outlast my lifespan, I will treasure those peacemaking opportunities to resolve conflict. If I want the "well done, good and faithful servant" from the Master, I will invest earthly gifts and wealth in the priorities of the Father while I'm here on earth. If I want the closeness of a spiritual community that is more secure and lasting than my family of origin, I will love generously my fellow prodigals that compose the body of Christ. Love is all about what you want. The question is, am I saying yes to the ways of love that will result in what I most deeply want?

I heard a story about Gary Player, the hall of fame golfer. As he was hitting a bucket of balls on the practice range, two passersby were watching. Every shot soared. Every swing was a study of fluidity. One of the observers muttered, "I'd give anything to be able to hit a three-iron like that." Mr. Player overheard the remark and turned to him. "Really? Would you give anything? Would you come out here every day and hit five hundred balls until your hands blistered and your back ached? Would you seek advice from a coach about your flaws? Would you take the risk that the investment of your practice would someday pay off? Really, would you give anything?"

How badly do you want the summit, the peak experience, the ultimate goal of life? What do you really want, and do you want it enough to do the work? Is it more than a fleeting wish or a temporary feeling? Love the way you want, really want, by saying yes to discerning the truth in every situation and acting in accordance with it. Love by saying yes to protecting that which is valuable and sacred, even when it happens to be packaged as a person who is disagreeable at the moment. Love by saying yes to trust when God calls for your investments, even when the immediate return is negligible. Love leans into hope and leans upon hope when adverse circumstances make you want to capitulate to despair. Love says yes to the long haul, the undaunted resilience of dogged perseverance. It never quits because it wants what God wants, and God never wears out.

As I write this, I'm witnessing the waltz of love by Dick and Bea Carlson. Married fifty-six years, he leads and she follows. He holds, and she trusts. He says yes to love and she says no to pride. Bea has progressive supranuclear palsy (PSP). Though fully cognizant mentally, her neurological condition is causing her to lose the connection with her world physically. There is no known treatment or medication for her condition. She has gone from walker to wheelchair, from soft food to pureed drinks, from slurred speech to eye movements. Hard end-of-life decisions loom. Dick and Bea are in this together.

But love keeps saying yes. And it's not a hesitant, grudging yes. Dick calls his twenty-four-hour care for his wife a "beautiful situation" because they are both cast daily into utter dependence on God's mercy. He never fails them. She has no fear, and he has no regret. Each day they "melt into moldability," in Dick's words, not fretting over what-ifs but surrendering gently to the process of the present. It takes an hour to feed Bea breakfast, another for lunch, and another for supper. Nothing can be hurried. Dick is physically taxed but spiritually energized. He experiences the very essence of God's presence every day and expresses concern that he not take pride in that intimacy. Humility and gratitude permeate his words.

Dick and Bea are sustained in part by these words of A. W. Tozer: "God wills that we should push into his presence and live our whole lives there. This is to be known to us in conscious experience. It is more than a doctrine to be held; it is a life to be enjoyed every moment of every day." Their lives have been stripped of all distraction, reduced to sharp focus. And what they are discovering and enjoying is that love never fails. It is their conscious experience from God and toward each other every day.

So love says yes to the needs of another and no to the desires of the moment, not out of sheer discipline but out of abundance. Love is supplied by the endless outpouring of God's loving presence into daily life. Love is invigorated by gratitude for gifts received here on earth and by endowments promised in heaven. Dick and Bea show that love truly and practically rejoices with the truth, always protects, always trusts, always hopes, and always perseveres. Their dance of humility and gratitude proves that love never fails.

When the apostle Paul wrote 1 Corinthians 13, he wasn't writing a wedding poem. He was writing to a real world church full of squabbling factions, competitive teachers, and rude behaviors. It was in this context that he summed up love's positive qualities as "kind." Paul is a realist. Love must flourish where it finds itself, not in some wished-for fantasy land.

Love starts in deep wanting, a wanting so palpable that daily schedules are reconfigured for the sake of demonstrating real love. This is a wanting that is so passionate it can risk the investment of love in an ungrateful teenager. This is a wanting of the summit so focused that it can't be stopped or daunted by the demandingness of the real people in your home, the office, or the neighborhood. Each unique individual is worthy of proactive investment. Each one is starving for this positive installment of love. And love will win out because there is nothing that compares with this view from the summit.

Add love to your repertoire of handholds. It's the next right thing. Love is the ultimate right thing. It's the climactic grip on God's goodness and the world's deepest desire. Do what you want. Aspire to the summit and see the horizon like you have never seen it before. Savor what has been given and the privilege to share it with others.

For personal application:

1. If you are married, what have you learned about loving another person that you didn't know prior to your wedding?

2. How have you learned to say "no" to certain reactions so that love is shown instead?

3. What do you want for your deepest relationships? What does that require?

4. What circumstance are you facing in your marriage where love is the next right thing to cling to?

5. When did someone do the next right thing and give the love that helped you hang on?

---

[1] Derek Lundy,Godforsaken Sea, (Chapel Hill, NC, Algonquin Books) p 159

10

Conclusion

The Promise

> For if you possess these qualities in
> increasing measure, *they will keep you from
> being ineffective and unproductive* in your
> knowledge of our Lord Jesus Christ.
>
> —2 Peter 1:8 (emphasis added)

What a legacy to leave. Everyone recognizes him, but not for his resume or for his written words, not for his family or his heroism, and certainly not because he has stood in the spotlight of fame and fortune. They recognize him by his boots: his neon-green climbing boots protruding from the snow, attached to his frozen body, not far from the summit of Mt. Everest. His name: Tsewang Paljor. He came from the far north of India and froze to death during the 1996 storm immortalized by Jon Krakauer's best-selling book *Into Thin Air*.

Virtually every climber of the North Face of Everest knows him only as "Green Boots," and not by his actual name. He has become a grim trail marker, and his final resting place a well-used rest stop for exhausted climbers on their way to the summit. For nearly twenty years, his frozen body has remained an irrefutable monument to failure and an unavoidable harbinger of danger. He summited, but the summit was his demise, not his success. Any climb that is not a round-trip is, by definition, a failure.

After all our talk of handholds and belays, and though the image of summiting is fresh in our minds, the stark reality remains: this is not a game. The stakes are high, and inattention can be costly. The tone of our mentor's instruction is positive and upward-looking, but it cannot eliminate the reminders of potential failure. Nobody wants to be Green Boots.

Jesus told parables that showed the seduction of chasing temporary success but losing sight of the ultimate objective, like summiting the mountain but not returning from the summit alive. One story tells of the rich man who lived in luxury but ignored the beggar named Lazarus who lay at his gate (Luke 16:19–31). Upon death the rich man found himself in hell, pleading for one drop of water from the fingertip of Lazarus. When it was too late, he finally recognized the importance of faith in God. Jesus told another story about the farmer (Luke 12:13–21) who tore down his barns to build bigger ones and found his pleasure in great accomplishment. But then his life was taken suddenly, and all his vast wealth proved totally irrelevant.

Perhaps the parable most apropos to this book's theme is the parable of the Wise and Foolish Builders (Luke 6:46–49). The story tells about two builders. One dug down to bedrock for his foundation. The other built quickly on the surface ground. Both houses experienced the same wind, rain, and floods. It was not as if one was spared testing and the other exempted. But the outcome was drastically different. One house stood, and the other utterly collapsed. And this is Jesus's cryptic and unforgettable point: "I will show you what he is like who comes to me and hears my words and puts them into practice" (Luke 6:47).

Peter, our mentor and coach, is faithful to bring the same invitation and the same warning. There is a promise in these concluding words (2 Pet. 1:8), but it comes with a not-so-subtle warning. The promise Peter makes is that doing the next right thing as a lifestyle, becoming proficient in the timely use of these handholds, will result in an effective and productive life. We will leave a legacy of fruitfulness by discovering through daily practice and proficiency that "His divine power has given us everything we need for life and godliness" (2 Pet. 1:3). But the warning reverberates through his words "ineffective" and "unproductive." The dark side is always there, unavoidably protruding from the snow: a forgotten name and only Green Boots as an epitaph. So there is a double incentive to do the next right thing.

Knowledge of the Lord Jesus Christ, fascination with sound doctrine, and increasing understanding of the Word will not result in a legacy of overcoming faith unless I practice what is needed under real world conditions as I find them.

> *Do not merely listen to the word, and so deceive yourselves. Do what it says. Anyone who listens to the word but does not do what it says is like a man who looks at his face in a mirror and, after looking at himself, goes away and immediately forgets what he looks like.*

*But the man who looks intently into the perfect law that
gives freedom, and continues to do this, not forgetting
what he has heard, but doing it—he will be blessed in
what he does. (James 1:22–27)*

Peter's counsel works. It works where faith meets life.
It works when havoc blows against the structures of our
lifestyle. It works where eternal promises meet street-level
challenges. It works in the office, the kitchen, the workshop,
or the hospital. His practical advice gives us a grip on
progress even when gravity, fear, and discouragement
dominate our environment. The promise is, do the next
right thing and you will outflank fear and overcome futility.
You will be effective and productive. But it isn't easy nor
automatic. Cold, harsh reality can blindside us. Even when
we think we are ready to face the challenge the process can
be daunting.

This is why we need mentors like Peter. Because we
are novices to crisis and neophytes to the battle we need
someone who has been here before. Mentors meet us in that
real world and not in the academic ivory tower. And this is
why Peter proves invaluable as our mentor. He speaks into
the process that seems to be taking too long. He takes our
hand when we are fatigued and body slammed. He points
out a next step when we are stuck. A mentor shows us the
progress we are making when we can't see it ourselves.

In these few verses, Peter reminds us of the promise,
a promise tailored for earth-bound, time-limited travelers.
God has given us everything we need (2 Pet. 1:3), but we
are to make every effort (v 5) to apply each handhold as
conditions require. "For if you do these things, you will
never fall…" (v 10). Do the next right thing. Make the next
decision the right one, even if it is not the ultimate one.

That decision has more to do with who you trust, and the development of your character than solving the problem you are facing. There is always the next right thing.